**30th ANNIVERSARY EDITION**

# The **45** SECOND
# **PRESENTATION**

## That Will Change **YOUR LIFE**

**UNDERSTANDING NETWORK MARKETING**

# DON FAILLA

MANJUL

**Manjul Publishing House**

*First published in India by*

**Manjul Publishing House Pvt. Ltd.**
• 2$^{nd}$ Floor, Usha Preet Complex,
42 Malviya Nagar, Bhopal 462 003 - India
• 7/32, Ground Floor, Ansari Road, Daryaganj, New Delhi 110 002
Email: manjul@manjulindia.com  Website: www.manjulindia.com

*Distribution Centres:*
Ahmedabad, Bengaluru, Bhopal, Kolkata, Chennai,
Hyderabad, Mumbai, New Delhi, Pune

This edition first published in 2013
Third impression 2014

**ISBN   978-81-8322-298-3**

Printed & bound in India by Thomson Press (India) Ltd.

This edition is authorised for sale in the following countries:
India, Bangladesh, Bhutan, Myanmar, Nepal, Pakistan and Sri Lanka

## ABOUT THE BOOK

There are already millions of people in Network Marketing and millions more coming in every year. The most important thing for a new person is to understand this business. You can spend four hours explaining it to them, or you can loan them this book.

## ABOUT THE AUTHOR

Don Failla started his network marketing career in 1967, He developed a proven system for building a large oranization by paying attention to what worked as he built his business. Today, Don and his wife Nancy travel worldwide teaching their proven system as international lifestyle trainers. They live in California, and they have two sons, - Doug and Greg, and five grandchildren. This book has sold millions of copies and is available in many languages. It is a major part of Don's proven system.

## DEDICATION

This book is dedicated to the Free Enterprise System of which we all have the opportunity to enjoy, and without which MLM would be impossible.

*"Withhold not good from them to whom it is due, when it is in the power of thine hand to do it."*

Bruce Vo
209-298-5868

# TABLE OF CONTENTS

# PREFACE

The 45-second presentation is all one needs to know to start building a large organization. In fact, if one cannot learn this presentation, they can read it to

---

The "45 Second Presentation" that will change your life.

**Q:** Have you ever thought about what it would be like to "Own Your Life"?

This is what I think it means to "Own Your Life"...
When you subtract out the sleeping time, commuting time, working time and things you have to do each and every day of your life, most people don't have more than one to two hours a day to do what they would like to do; and then, would they have the money to do it?

We have discovered a way a person can learn how to "Own their Life" by building a home-based business; and we have a system for doing it that is so simple anyone can do it. It doesn't require selling, and the best part is, it won't take much of your time. If you are interested, contact the person who gave you this book.

---

a friend or put it on a 3 x 5 card and let their friends read it for themselves.

Beyond this presentation you do not need to know anything. Once you realize this and understand, you can introduce your business to anyone, because absolutely anyone can build a business if they want to. All they really need is a little desire. Without desire, you have nothing.

The secret to the system we teach is not to talk. Talking is your worst enemy.

The more you talk the more the prospect thinks they cannot do what you are doing. The more you talk, the more they think they don't have time. Remember time is the number one excuse people have for not getting started.

After your friend reads the 45-second presentation they may ask you a question. Regardless of what the question is, if you answer it you lose. They will have five more questions before you know it. You will be bouncing all over the place! Simply tell them that they will have a lot of questions and that the system is designed to answer most of them. Have them read the first four Napkin presentations and then get back to you.

Never tell the prospect to read the book. They will set it on the shelf and get to it in due time. Tell them to read the first four Napkin presentations. They will read it right away and over 90% will finish the book at the same time.

After reading the book, your prospect will understand network marketing. This is important because the number one reason people don't do the business is because they don't understand it. Now they will understand network marketing, and they will be ready for you to present your vehicle, company, products and marketing plan. But I said you don't have to know anything other than the 45-second presentation to get started. So now what do you do?

At this point you would use the tools or your team to do the talking for you. Tools would be brochures, audio tapes and video tapes from your company. Your team would be your immediate up-line starting with the person who will be your sponsor.

Let's say you have your first prospect! You have done the 45-second presentation and they have read the book. You invite your prospect to meet you for lunch. Let them know you will also be inviting your sponsor who can explain the business on your behalf.

(Key point - Who pays for lunch? You do. Your sponsor is working for you. How many times would you have to buy your sponsor lunch or dinner before you could explain the business on your own?)

We had a man come up to us at a seminar in Germany and say "Not only do you not need to know anything to get started, you could also have a free lunch every day when you are working for your downline."

Happy eating and watch your business grow!

# CHAPTER 1
## Introduction To MLM

MULTI-LEVEL MARKETING is one of the fastest growing yet most misunderstood methods of moving products in use today. It has been termed by many as the Thing-of-the Nineties. Believe me; it will go far beyond that. By 2010 more than 200 BILLION DOLLARS worth of products and services will be moving annually through Multi-Level Marketing companies. WATCH OUT for MLM in the 21st century!

The purpose of this book is to convey to you, the reader, through illustrations and examples, just what Multi-Level Marketing IS and what it IS NOT. We will also show you how you can effectively, I repeat-EFFECTIVELY, explain Multi-Level Marketing to others.

This book should be treated as a TRAINING MANUAL. It is intended to be used as a tool to help you train the people in your organization. Include it in their initial "kit" of information about your program.

I developed the "Napkin presentations," upon which this book is based, in 1973. I have been involved in Multi-Level Marketing to one degree or another since 1969. This book will cover the 10 presentations developed thus far.

Before going into the details of the "Ten Napkin presentations," allow me to answer one of the most frequently asked, and probably the most basic of all the questions, "What is MLM?" This question is asked quite frequently in response to a button we often wear. Throughout this book we shall use "MLM" and "Multi-Level Marketing" interchangeably.

Let's break it down. Marketing simply means moving a product or service from the manufacturer or provider to the consumer. Multi-Level refers to the system of compensation provided to those persons who are causing the product to move or the service to be provided. "Multi" means "more than one." "Level" refers to what may better be termed as, "generation." It could be called "Multi-Generation Marketing." We will stay with Multi-Level since that is what is most common. It is so common, in fact, that many illegal pyramids and chain distribution schemes or chain-letters try to pass themselves off as being Multi-Level programs. This creates such a stigma, although unjustified, that many of the newer MLM companies are using other names for their type of marketing. Some of the names you will hear are "Uni-Level Marketing," "Network Marketing," and "Co-op Mass Marketing."

There are really only three basic methods of moving products. (Hold up three fingers as you demonstrate this point.)

1) RETAILING—I'm sure everyone is familiar with retailing. The grocery store, the drug store, the department store. Going into a store and buying something is retail.

2) DIRECT SALES—would usually, (but not always) include insurance, cookware, encyclopedias, etc. Fuller Brush, the Avon lady, Tupperware home parties, etc. are some examples of Direct Sales efforts.

3) MULTI-LEVEL MARKETING—MLM is the one we will be discussing in this book. It should not be confused with the other two, especially with the Direct Sales method with which MLM commonly is confused.

A fourth type of marketing that is sometimes added to the list (hold up the fourth finger) is MAIL ORDER. Mail Order can be an MLM type, but most generally is included in the Direct Sales category.

A fifth type, often confused with MLM, I have already mentioned is PYRAMID SALES. The fact is, PYRAMIDS are ILLEGAL! One of the main reasons they are illegal is their failure to move a product or to provide a valid service. If a product doesn't move, how can you even call it "marketing," let alone "Multi-Level Marketing!" Multi-Level they may be–but MARKETING THEY ARE NOT!!!

Most objections that people have about getting into Multi-Level Marketing are due to not realizing the differences between MLM and the Direct Sales methods of marketing. This confusion is understandable because most reputable MLM companies belong to the Direct Selling Association.

You have been conditioned, perhaps, to think of them as door-to-door direct sales programs because your first encounter with them was when a distributor knocked on your door to sell you something.

There are some features that differentiate MLM from Retail and Direct Sales companies. One very significant difference is that in MLM you are in business for yourself—BUT NOT BY YOURSELF.

By being in business for yourself, whether or not but especially if you are operating out of your home, you may be entitled to some substantial TAX BREAKS. We won't get into TAX ADVANTAGES in this book. Most people can get that information from their accountant or from the many books that have been written on the subject.

Being in business for yourself, you are buying the products wholesale from the company you are representing. This means that you can (and should) use these items for your own consumption. Many people get involved in a company at first for this reason alone, to buy wholesale. And many of those will get "serious."

Since you are buying your products at WHOLESALE, you can, if you wish to, sell those products at RETAIL and make a PROFIT. The most common misunderstanding about MLM is the notion that you HAVE TO sell retail to be successful. There is a lot to be said for selling retail and it should not be ignored. Some programs even require that a retail quota be met in order to qualify for a bonus. You may sell if you want to or have to due to your particular program's requirements, but in regard to making the larger sums of income-the real success is in building the organization.

IMPORTANT POINT: Let your sales come as the natural result of building the organization. More people fail than succeed by trying to do it the other way around—they try to build the organization by emphasizing selling. As you read through the Napkin presentations that follow, you will see this concept unfold before you.

The word "selling" triggers negative thoughts in the minds of about 95% of the people. In MLM you don't need to "sell" the products in the traditional sense of the word. However, PRODUCT DOES HAVE TO MOVE or nobody, but nobody, gets paid. I define selling as "calling on strangers and trying to sell them something they may neither need nor want." Again, PRODUCT HAS TO MOVE OR NOBODY GETS PAID!

Another name for MLM is Network Marketing. When you build an organization, you are actually building a network through which you can channel your products. Retailing is the foundation of Network Marketing. Sales in MLM or Network Marketing come from distributors SHARING with their friends, neighbors, and relatives. They never have to talk to strangers.

To build a LARGE SUCCESSFUL BUSINESS, you need a BALANCE. You need to sponsor and teach MLM, and in the process of doing this you can build a customer base by retailing to your friends, neighbors, and relatives.

Don't try to sell the world on your program yourself. Remember that Network Marketing or MLM is building an organization in which a lot of distributors retail a little. This is far better than a few trying to do it all.

With virtually all MLM companies, the need to spend large sums of money on advertising is non-existent. Advertising is done almost exclusively by word-of-mouth. For this reason they have more money to put into product development. As a result, they usually have a higher quality product than their counterpart found in retail stores. You can SHARE with a friend a high quality product of a type that they are already using. You're simply replacing their old brand with something that you have discovered through your own experience to be better.

So you see, its not going door-to-door every day calling on strangers. All network or MLM programs that I know of teach that if you simply SHARE the quality of their products or services with friends, that is all the "selling" that is involved. (I prefer to call it "Sharing," because that's what it is!)

Another thing that differentiates MLM from Direct Sales is the SPONSORING of other distributors. In direct sales, and even in some MLM companies, it's called RECRUITING. However, "sponsoring" and "recruiting" are definitely not the same thing. You SPONSOR someone then

TEACH them how to do what you are doing–building a BUSINESS OF THEIR OWN.

I emphasize that there is a big difference between sponsoring someone and just "signing them up." When you SPONSOR someone, you are making a COMMITMENT to them. If you are not willing to make that commitment, then you are doing them a disservice by signing them up.

At this point, all you need to be is WILLING to help them build a business of their own. This book will be an invaluable tool in showing you what and how to do just that.

It is a RESPONSIBILITY of a sponsor to teach the people they bring into a business all they know about that business. Things such as: how to order products and keep records, how to get started, how to build and train their organization, etc. This book will go a long way toward making you ABLE to meet that responsibility.

SPONSORING is what makes a Multi-Level Marketing business grow. As your organization grows, you are building toward becoming an INDEPENDENT, SUCCESSFUL businessperson. You are your OWN BOSS!

With Direct Selling companies, you work for the company. If you decide to quit that company and move to another area, you end up having to start all over again. In almost all of the MLM programs that I am aware of, you can move to another area of the country and sponsor people without losing the volume generated by the group you left behind.

In Multi-Level Marketing programs you can make a lot of money. It takes a little longer with some companies than it does with others, but making a lot of money comes from building an organization, not by just selling the product. To be sure, you can make a good living in some programs by just selling the product–but you can make a FORTUNE by building an organization as your primary function.

People will get started in a Multi-Level business with the idea of making $50, $100, or even $200 per month and suddenly they will realize that if they want to get serious about the business they could be making $1,000 or $2,000 per month–or more. Again, remember that a person doesn't make that kind of money by just selling the products...they make that kind of money by building an organization.

THAT IS THE PURPOSE OF THIS BOOK: to teach you the things you need to know to be able to build an organization and to build it FAST–to develop certain and proper attitudes about MLM. If a person thinks Multi-Level Marketing is illegal, having a connotation of being like a pyramid (and they do make that comparison), you are going to have trouble sponsoring them.

You must teach them the facts to eliminate their attitude of mistaking a true Multi-Level Marketing organization for a pyramid. One example you could show them is the illustration on the next page. The pyramid is built from the top down and only those in at the very beginning can ever be near the top.

In the "MLM" triangle, everybody starts at the bottom and has the opportunity to build a large organization.

A new person can build an organization many times larger than his sponsor's organization if he wants.

The main objective is to get your prospect into a general discussion concerning MLM and explain with your three fingers the differences between Retailing, Direct Sales, and Multi-Level Marketing. Then you will have a good start at sponsoring them into your particular MLM vehicle.

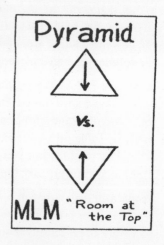

As I stated earlier, by the 2010, MLM will be doing in excess of $200 BILLION annually. That is BIG BUSINESS!

Most people don't realize that MLM is that big! Multi-Level Marketing has been in our midst for over 50 years! Some companies have been around for over 45 years and are already doing a billion dollars per year by themselves.

I know of one company that did over $6.5 million in its first year of operation. In its second year it made over $62 MILLION. For their third year they projected $122 MILLION. They are on track to hit ONE BILLION per year by their 10th year. The principles expounded in this book will make that goal reachable. That's a pretty fast start in anybody's league!

MULTI-LEVEL MARKETING is one of the viable ways for an inventor or manufacturer to put a new product on the market without having a million dollars and without having to totally give up their product to someone else.

# NOTES

# CHAPTER 2
## Napkin Presentation #1
## Two Times Two Is Four

THIS one you can show a person BEFORE they see the program or the vehicle you want to share with them. It is an absolute MUST to show them this presentation as soon after you have introduced them to your program as you can. You want their thinking to be going in the right direction from day one. What this will do is take the proverbial "Monkey off their Back" in thinking they have to go out and "sponsor the world" to make a large amount of money in Multi-Level Marketing.

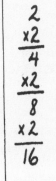

This presentation will also show them how important it is to work with their people and help them to get started.

This presentation starts by your writing down "2 x 2 is 4," etc., and multiplying on down as shown in the figure on the right.

I tell a joke on people, that if they sponsor someone who can't do this right here-PASS-because you are going to have trouble working with them.

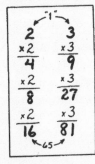

Notice that we start using the word "sponsor" now. To the right of the 2 x 2 column, write 3 x 3 saying, "Over here you sponsor three people, and you teach (We also start to use the word "teach") these 3 to sponsor three, making nine more. Then you teach your 3 people how to teach those 9 to sponsor and now you have 27. Going on down 1 more level, you will have 81. Notice the difference between 16 and 81. Bring it to their attention and ask them if they would agree that it's a pretty good difference. Then point out to them the REAL DIFFERENCE is ONE! Everybody only sponsored ONE MORE! You will usually pick up some reaction from this, but continue right on–it gets better.

Let's say you sponsor 4 people into the business. Moving to the right of the 3 x 3 column, you again run down a column of figures, writing them down as you speak.

"Let's see what happens if everybody sponsored only TWO MORE." As you continue to write, say, "You sponsor 4 and teach them to sponsor 4. Then you help your 4 to teach the 16 they have to sponsor 4, adding 64 to your group. Working down only one more level, and before you know it, your group has 256 more."

And again you point out, "Now that's getting to be a considerable difference right there, but the..."

You will usually catch some sort of reaction again as they begin to pick up on the concept, and cutting in they will say before you do, "The REAL DIFFERENCE is that everybody only sponsored TWO MORE!"

We end it with five. They will usually pick up on it by now and mentally or verbally follow right along with you as you write in the final column of figures. By now you can leave out "sponsoring" and "teaching," writing down the figures and commenting, "5 times 5 is 25, times 5 is 125, times 5 is 625. Now that is a FANTASTIC DIFFERENCE!" Again, the REAL DIFFERENCE is that everybody only had to sponsor THREE more.

Most people can relate to sponsoring 1, 2, or 3 more, but usually find it difficult to relate to the figures on the bottom line. (16, 81, 256, and 625).

So picture yourself in the last column, having had the time to sponsor 5 serious people into the program. The "5" at the top of the column represents the ones you sponsored who want to get SERIOUS about building a business of their own. You may have to sponsor 10, 15 or 20 people to get these 5.

However, once you totally understand all ten of the NAPKIN PRESEN-TATIONS, you will find that your people will get serious QUICKER than people who come into organizations that don't know this material. This book will teach you how to work with them so they will get serious QUICKER.

Notice in the figure at the right, that when you have sponsored five, and they have sponsored five, and so forth, right on down the line ... you add all these (circled figures) up and you will have 780 serious people in your organization. Doing this will help you answer the question, "Doesn't somebody have to sell the product?" You've all heard that question before if you've been at all active. So just go through this NAPKIN PRESENTATION with them and explain that 2 times 2 is 4...right on up to 780 distributors.

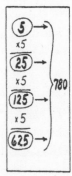

In ANY KIND of Multi-Level Marketing organization, if you have 780 people just USING the product themselves, you have a tremendous volume. (And we haven't even included those which are not serious but are just "product buyers.")

Now if they all have 2, 3, 4, or 5 friends...let's just say they all had 10 customers from among their friends, relatives, and acquaintances, that's 7,800 customers! Add to that the 780 distributors in your organization-do you think 8,580 customers plus the "product buyers" will be able to provide you with a profitable enterprise? That's how you make a lot of money in any business—by having a lot of people doing a little bit. But remember, you are only working with 5 SERIOUS PEOPLE, not a whole army!

We run into people constantly in other MLM programs, as well as our own, who are amazed at how FAST our own organizations have grown. They have been in their programs longer than we have, but are scratching the "think tank" on top of their necks and asking, "What are you doing that I'm not doing?"

Our response to them is, "How many people in your FRONT LINE are you working with?" (The Front Line are those people directly sponsored by you. They are also called your "first level" distributors.)

I will usually hear figures anywhere from 25 to 50 or more. I know people in MLM who have over 100 in their front line, and I'll guarantee you, that once you understand the principles outlined in this book, you'll pass those people up in six months, even though they have been in their organizations for 6-8 years.

As we go into Napkin presentation #2 covering the "Salesman Failure Syndrome in Multi-Level Marketing, I will give you a simple parallel showing why having so many front line people isn't good.

Consider the ARMY, the NAVY, the AIR FORCE, the MARINES, or the COAST GUARD. From the lowest private up to the top brass in the Pentagon, nobody has more than 5 or 6 people they are trying to DIRECTLY supervise. (There may be rare exceptions.) Think about it! Here we have West Point and Annapolis with over 200 years of experience each, and they don't think anybody should supervise more than 5 or 6 people. So you tell me why people get into a Multi-Level Marketing organization and think they can effectively work with 50 people in their front line. They CAN'T DO IT! That's why a lot of them fail, and you'll see why as you read on.

You shouldn't try to work with more than 5 serious people at a time. However, make sure that when you sponsor them, you start working downgroup. There is a point when they won't need you and they can break away and start another line on their own. This will also free you up to work with yet another serious person, keeping your number of those that you are working closely with at 5. Some programs may allow you to be effective with only 3 or 4 at a time, but none that I know of can be effectively built with more than 5.

These NAPKIN PRESENTATIONS tie together, so some of the questions you may have at this point will be cleared up as you read on.

# NOTES

# NOTES

# CHAPTER 3
## Napkin Presentation #2
## Salesmen Failure Syndrome

WHY do so many salesmen fail when working in a Multi-Level Marketing business? This #2 presentation will clarify the common mistakes made by sales-oriented professionals.

Let me explain why we would rather sponsor ten teachers than ten salesmen.

Now DON'T GET ME WRONG. I think professional salesmen can be a tremendous asset to your organization—if, like everyone else, they go through the 10 Napkin presentations and thoroughly understand them.

Most people get confused by the statement above, but remember, they still don't understand that MLM is a METHOD of marketing. We are NOT sponsoring people into a Direct Sales organization. We ARE sponsoring them into a Multi-Level Marketing program.

Much of the time, the problem you will have with a salesman is that when they see the high quality of the products you represent, they just launch out and take off, so to speak. They can put their own presentation together—they don't need us to tell them how to sell; they're the professional. The point is: we don't want to tell them how to sell. We just want to teach them how to TEACH and SPONSOR and build a large successful Multi-Level Marketing organization. And they, and anyone for that matter, can do just that WITHOUT SELLING ANYTHING in the normal sense and definition of the word "selling."

If you can't sit down with them and explain a few simple things about Multi-Level Marketing and why it is different than Direct Selling, the tendency is for them to go off in the wrong direction. As we continue on with the Napkin presentations, we will give you a few examples.

Most people think (and especially salesmen) that if you sponsor someone, you have duplicated your effort. (Draw one circle under the other.) There was one, and now there are two. It sounds logical, but that's NOT TRUE.

The reason it's not true is that if the one represented by the top circle (sponsor) goes away, the one they sponsored will go away also; they won't continue on. You must explain to your people that if they truly want to duplicate themselves, they have to be at least THREE LEVELS DEEP; only then are they DUPLICATED.

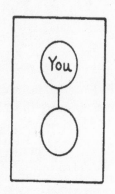

If your sponsor dropped out before you had an opportunity to see that the program really will work, you most likely will assume that it doesn't because it didn't for him. After all, he's your sponsor and certainly must know more about it than you. Let's say that you're here. (Draw a circle and put "YOU" in the middle of it.) You sponsor Tom. (Draw another circle under the one with "YOU" in it, write "TOM" in it, and connect the circles with a line.) Now, if you leave and Tom doesn't know what to do (because you haven't taught him), then that's the end of it. But if you DO TEACH Tom how to sponsor, and he sponsors Carol, you are ONLY BEGINNING to duplicate yourself.

But if Tom DOESN'T learn how to teach Carol to Sponsor, then again it will fizzle out and that's the end of it. You have to teach Tom HOW TO TEACH Carol how to sponsor. Then she can sponsor Betty or whomever.

Now you are THREE DEEP If you go away (to work with someone else or to a different area of the country), this sub-group will continue on. I emphasize: YOU HAVE TO GO THREE DEEP! You have nothing until you are three deep, and only then are you DUPLICATED.

If you never communicate anything but this one point to the people you sponsor, then you will have the key that will make you more successful than most others in Multi-Level Marketing programs.

Here's what happens to the "salesman": he looks at the demonstrations of the products, hears or reads of the testimonials of the results others have had with their use, and how they work. Armed with this information, just get out of his way, and he will go out and "sell like crazy." Remember, they're SALESMEN! They have been in the Direct Selling business, and they don't have any problem calling on strangers.

Great! So you say to your super-salesman (let's call him Charlie), "Charlie, if you want to make the BIG BUCKS, you cannot do it by yourself. You need to sponsor people."

So what does Charlie do? He goes out and sponsors, sponsors, sponsors... He will just sponsor up a storm. A good "salesman" in a Multi-Level Marketing program could sponsor 3 or 4 people per week.

But here is what happens: It gets to a point, (and it doesn't take long), that people are dropping out as fast as they are being added. If you don't work with them EFFECTIVELY (and you can't be effective if you are trying to work with more than five at a time), you will see them becoming discouraged and giving up.

So Charlie, being discouraged and a little bit impatient, doesn't think anything is happening, and he goes off to look for something else to sell. The person who sponsored Charlie, thinking Charlie was going to make them rich, gets discouraged and gives up also.

Most people who have made it big in MLM don't have a sales background. They may not be TEACHERS professionally, but most of them come from a background with an element of teaching in it. I know of one teacher, and school principal who after only 24 months in a Multi-Level Marketing program, was earning in excess of FIFTEEN THOUSAND DOLLARS PER MONTH. He did it and is doing it by TEACHING OTHERS how to do it also.

Let's put some numbers in Charlie's approach so we can more clearly see where he went wrong. We will assume that Charlie, being the super-salesman that he is, went out and sponsored 130 people. Let's also say that he got each of them to sponsor five others, adding 650 more for a total of 780 in his organization. (Sound familiar?)

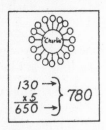

Ask your people this question when you show this to them, "Which do you feel you could do more quickly, sponsor five people who are serious and TEACH THEM HOW TO TEACH, or...?"

Incidentally, the question will come up, "What do I teach them?" The answer is; you teach them what you are learning right here in this book-the 10 NAPKIN PRESENTATIONS. They need to have an understanding of all ten, but initially the first four will work.

Teach them that 2 x 2 = 4, and why people fail, etc. How long do you think it would take you to sponsor 130 people? How many of the first ones would be left when you sponsored number 130? You would find that you are losing them pretty fast. Yet you will discover the retention rate on the 780 in Napkin presentation #1 to be quite high.

Once you show this to a salesman and the salesman understands it, they will say, 'Aha! Now I see what I've got to do...and they will go do it.

CAUTION: You must hold them back. Because they don't understand what we have just gone over in this chapter, most people in MLM will literally encourage their people right out of the business! They will sponsor someone and their new distributor will come to them and say, "Hey, I got five new people last week!" So you say, "Great!" and encouragingly slap them on the back. The following week they sign up five more people. What has become of the five they signed up the first week? They're gone.

If you understand this "Salesmen Failure Syndrome," you can still encourage them, but at the same time stress the point of how IMPORTANT it is to take those first five you sponsored and HELP THEM GET STARTED.

After I have sponsored someone, it's more important for me to go with them and HELP THEM SPONSOR someone else, than it is for me to go out and sponsor another person for myself. I just cannot emphasize this point too much. This point will come up again in a couple of other presentations.

Of the 10 Napkin presentations, the first four are really a MUST. If you don't have time for all of them, at least get started with #1 and #2. (Chap. 2 & 3). You can show them to someone, depending on how much you elaborate, in as quickly as five to ten minutes, once you have practiced them.

In one of the programs I was involved in, I sponsored this fellow named Carl. Carl told me about sponsoring his daughter in Tennessee, and that she knew everybody in town. I was talking to Carl on the phone and related to him that I thought it was great. I quickly added, however, that I needed to tell him something to pass on to his daughter. I asked him if he had a piece of paper and pencil handy (which he did) and I had him write down 2 x 2 is 4, and right on through it. I instructed him to immediately phone his daughter and let her know the mistakes to avoid to get her started in the right direction. He did call her, and it's working out very well for both of them.

# NOTES

# CHAPTER 4
## Napkin Presentation #3
## "Four Things You Have To Do"

IN THE FIRST PRESENTATION we told you some of the things TO DO, and in the second presentation we told you some things NOT TO DO, as far as working in depth with your organization. In this Napkin presentation we will show you four things you HAVE TO DO to be successful in an MLM program. These 4 things are an absolute MUST!

Everybody in Multi-Level Marketing who is making $100,000 or $200,000 per year (and more), DID and IS DOING these four things.

To help you remember these four things, I have paralleled the points to a story which you can relate to your people. They will not only pick up on the parallel, but will REMEMBER the "Have to do's" also.

The way the story goes is this: "Let's imagine you want to take a trip in the family car and leave rainy Washington (it really isn't as bad as some people like to make it out to be) and drive to sunny California. The sunshine in

California will represent reaching the top in the program that you're in. When you get there you are SUCCESSFUL–you're AT THE TOP!

The FIRST thing you have to do is GET IN and GET STARTED. There isn't anybody in MLM who has made a lot of money unless they first got started. The amount of money it takes to get started depends on the company and the program you choose as your "vehicle". It can range from nothing on up to $12.50, $45, $100, $200, or even $500 or more.

The SECOND THING you need to do as you take this trip is buy GAS and OIL. As you travel to the top (California), you will use up the fuel and oil (Products), and it will be necessary to replace them. MLM works best with products that are CONSUMABLE. You will use the products up and buy them again and again. You must USE THE PRODUCTS of the company you represent YOURSELF.

Remember, we showed you in N.P. #1, that with 780 distributors it doesn't matter which program you are in, you will have a very sizable volume. Naturally, you can see the advantages of building a business with a vehicle that has consumable products. Most Multi-Level companies are in that category. Non-consumables are usually marketed through retail or direct sales methods, but not always.

The other result of using the products yourself is you will get excited about them. Rather than spend a large sum of money on advertising, MLM companies put their money into product development, and as a result will usually have a higher quality product than that which is normally available in a retail store.

The THIRD thing you have to do is get into HIGH GEAR. Of course you realize that nobody starts out in HIGH gear. We all start out in NEUTRAL. (Incidentally, notice that we are not driving an "automatic.") We may be in the car, still in the driveway, with the key turned on and the mo-

tor racing, but if we never get out of neutral we will never get to California–or anywhere else for that matter.

To get your car into gear, you must sponsor someone into the business. When you sponsor someone, you are in FIRST GEAR. I believe you should be  in first gear five times, with 5 SERIOUS people. In one of the other presentations I show you how to determine which of your people are serious. You will want

your five people to get into gear ALSO. You TEACH them how to get into first gear by sponsoring someone. When each of your 5 people is in first gear 5 times, you will be in SECOND GEAR 25 times.

Teach your five people to teach their five to get into first gear five times. They are now in second gear 25 times each, and that puts you in THIRD GEAR 125 times. When you have third level distributors in your organization, you are in THIRD GEAR.

Have you noticed how much smoother your car runs in 4th gear? So does your organization! You want to be in HIGH GEAR (4th Gear) as soon as you can. When your first levels are in 3rd gear, you will be in FOURTH GEAR.

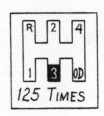

Naturally, you want your people to be in HIGH or FOURTH GEAR as well, and when they are, you are in OVERDRIVE.

How do you get into OVERDRIVE? YOU simple HELP TEACH the people you sponsored to get their people into THIRD GEAR, which puts them into 4th gear and puts you in OVERDRIVE.

The FOURTH THING, while you are on your journey to California, is to use the time you have to SHARE your products with the people who are going with you. Let them try them. Let them experience the benefits of the products. When they want to know where they can get them...guess what you do at that point? So share with your friends. For a number of people, this is the retailing part of the business.

At this point it is important to notice that as we went through Napkin presentations #1 and #2, and now here at #3, we've told you the FOUR THINGS YOU HAVE TO DO to be successful. Not once did we tell you that you HAVE TO go out and SELL. We say you don't have to sell the products in the normal sense of the word "sell". We DO SAY you need to SHARE the products with your friends. You can even share them with strangers. When they see the benefits of your products and your marketing plan, they will become NEW FRIENDS.

You don't even need a large number of customers...say 10, or even less. If all you ever had was 10 customers...hey, that's okay. All it means is item number 4 (next page) is a very small portion. So what if we cover up the "4" altogether–you could still get to California by doing the first three.

1. GET IN — GET STARTED
2. USE THE PRODUCTS
3. SHIFT INTO HIGH GEAR
4. SHARE WITH FRIENDS (RETAIL)

NOTICE, HOWEVER: If you didn't do number 3 (get into HIGH GEAR) and did a lot of number 4, you would never get out of the driveway. (That's what salesmen do.) Once you understand this and tie it in with #1 and #2, you start developing the proper MLM attitude.

Starting from square one with your new person, you want to get into their sub-conscious the NUMBER "5". All you need to do is find 5 serious people who want to get serious about the business.

When you run into people and ask them how they are doing, you may hear the response, "Gee, I can't find anyone who wants to sell." There's that word "sell" again! QUIT LOOKING for people who want to sell! START LOOKING for people who want to earn an extra $600, $1,200, or $1,500 per month without having to "go to work" everyday. Do you or they know anybody like that? Your answer and theirs, like mine, will be, "Yeah-everybody!" Well those are the people you want to talk to, because everybody would like to have that kind of dough coming in.

Simply point out that it may take 5 to 10 hours a week of their spare time to build a business. But then we hasten to say, "What's wrong with that?"

People sometimes get into MLM programs and think somehow it's all going to happen just because they signed up. Not so! Remember, the car we are driving to California does NOT have an AUTOMATIC transmission.

I know, and surely you know, people who have gone to college to get a degree, and there is absolutely nothing wrong with that. Maybe you're one of them. You go to school everyday. You study all day and half the night, week after week, for YEARS. Then, when you finally graduate–how much money can you make?

So give 5 to 10 hours of your time each week to LEARNING the 10 Napkin presentations and everything you can about the MLM company you are representing. When you learn and understand them, you can teach the Napkin presentations to others. The book you are now reading is your key to tomorrow's success.

We don't want you to get uptight by thinking you can't teach someone what you are learning here. Sure, this may be the first time you've read or heard these concepts, and we really can't expect you to know it all well enough to teach it. But then you DON'T HAVE TO!

Remember, to get into a Multi-Level Marketing program, you have to have a SPONSOR. If your sponsor is a REAL "sponsor", he will help you with your first 5 people. Notice: It's a HELPING RELATIONSHIP. In the process of showing the Napkin presentations to your friends at meetings (one-on-one or groups), your sponsor is training you as well.

As a suggestion, we ask that you set some sort of goal for yourself. When you are about 20% up the ladder in your program, you should KNOW and UNDERSTAND the ten NAPKIN PRESENTATIONS. By the time you get 3/4 of the way, you should be able to TEACH others. When you are at or near the top, you will be able TO TEACH your people TO TEACH others. It's something beneficial that you can MASTER over a relatively short period of time.

With this book and/or the CD on the same subject, you can sit down and read and study, or listen to the CD again and again and again. If you were given an "assignment" to do the above, and you had to go through the material 5, 6, or even 10 times, and a year from now it meant you could be making 2, 3, 4, or even 6 THOUSAND DOLLARS A MONTH, is it worth spending five to ten hours a week?

Now you have to admit, that's a pretty neat way to "go to school", right? Take a look at some of those college textbooks and trying to learn what they contain; they're not going to make that kind of money for you!

## *Welcome to MLM University!*

### FOUR THINGS YOU HAVE TO DO

1. Get in — Get Started
2. Use the Products
3. Shift into High Gear
4. Share with friends (Retail)

# NOTES

# NOTES

# CHAPTER 5
## Napkin Presentation #4
## Digging Down To Bedrock

DISCOURAGEMENT is one of the problems that can beset a new distributor you have sponsored if you fail to impress upon them the importance of getting a HEAD START. That is why we stress that they DO NOT START COUNTING their months-in-the-business until they have had their TRAINING MONTH or their Training Period of whatever length of time they need.

When they first get into an MLM organization, they may have a tendency, without a HEAD START, to look up at the leaders way out in front and become discouraged and think they will never be able to catch up.

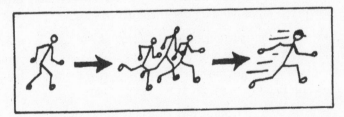

Draw a picture of a crowd of runners. Note the arrows showing a runner trying to catch up to the crowd-and the runner going even FASTER trying to stay ahead of the others. (You may find it simpler to draw circles to illustrate this point.) Remember when you were in PE in school and were running "Laps?" People will run faster to stay ahead of a crowd than to catch up to it. Since there is no "Finish Line" in this race, you can all be winners. I have a quote from my pastor that I display in my office. It reads:

### *"THE ONLY LOSERS ARE THE QUITTERS"*

However, to run a good race, one should train for it. When you sponsor someone, have them consider the first 2 to 6 weeks in the business as their training month. The NEXT month will be their STARTING month.

Everything they read or listen to, meetings they attend, getting together with their sponsor and other people, the products they try, and the products they move—all this TRAINING is giving them a HEAD START on their STARTING MONTH in the business, which is NEXT MONTH. When next month comes, if they're not yet ready to get serious about the program, consider that they are still in their TRAINING MONTH or period. Don't have them start counting their months until they are ready to get serious. That way, when they finally do get serious, they will be "warmed up" for the race and can get off to a HEAD START and a FASTER RACE.

One of the major benefits of all these Napkin presentations is that as you share them with your new distributors and prospects and have training programs, they have a tendency to become SELF MOTIVATORS. Every time I show the "2 x 2 is 4" presentation, I get all excited again about the possibilities in MLM.

Once you read and study and understand what I am going to show you in the following pages, you will be motivated and encouraged every time you see a new high rise office building under construction.

Notice that when construction begins it seems like it takes months and months, almost forever, before you see it begin to rise out of the ground. But once it gets above ground-level it seems to rise about one floor per week—it goes up FAST!

So picture that tall office building as your own organization as it will be SOMEDAY, and ponder what you will have to do to get it.

When you first began to sponsor those first five serious people, you were digging the foundation with a SHOVEL or a SPADE.

But notice that when you dig down into the second level by teaching your people to sponsor, that's 25 people now, and you have to bring in the BULL-DOZERS.

When you have taught your people how to teach the people in their group to sponsor, you are well on your way to bedrock and you are now beginning to excavate with STEAM SHOVELS! When you have begun to see the 125 third level people, you have reached BEDROCK.

Now you can start going up. When you are down FOUR DEEP in your organization, it means you are now starting to "become visible," and your building will rise up quite rapidly.

So, if you have been in the business for several months and don't see anything happening, don't get discouraged. It's just that the foundation is still under construction. It's sort of like the gold prospector who spent months and months digging a mine, only to give up and quit when he was just 6 inches from the main vein.

Again, let's go back to the salesman. That's what happens to them. They move on to something else just as they were about to hit bedrock and start seeing the building rise. You really can't expect to see visible results of real growth until you have gone down at least 4-deep. It doesn't necessarily mean you have to be 5-deep AND 4-deep. If any one of your lines is four deep it means you are starting to build floors and are visible.

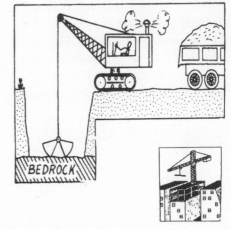

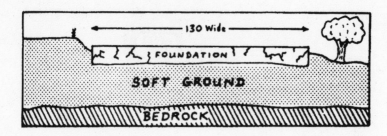

Above is an illustration of what the foundation of the person that sponsors 130 will look like. Notice that they haven't reached bedrock even if they each sponsored 5 "product-users" or "wholesale-buyers" and had a group of 780. Without a solid foundation sitting on bedrock, the building can't get too tall or it will crumble.

Relating this back to taking a trip to California, the person that sponsored 130 was in first gear too many times. If they all sponsored 5, he would never get out of second gear!

LEARN these Napkin presentations and USE THEM! You won't get stuck in Second-Gear. Build your foundation deep, down to BEDROCK, and you'll reach HIGH GEAR!

When we get to Napkin presentation #9 (Chapter 10) on Motivation and Attitude, and the other presentations, you will thoroughly understand why it's important to BUILD DEEP. Before going to N.P. #5, I want to remind you that you should show your people the first four presentations AS SOON AS POSSIBLE. The ones that follow can be introduced any time after your people have started sponsoring others into the business.

# NOTES

# NOTES

# CHAPTER 6
## Napkin Presentation #5
## Ships At Sea

YOU have now been in your business for about a week, two weeks, a month, or whatever length of time it takes for you to decide to get serious and get GROWING. By this time you have sponsored a number of people.

This presentation is one that is fun to do with a group of people, more so than in a one-on-one situation.

Almost everybody has heard the phrase, "When MY ship comes in..." I'm reminded of the pessimist who flippantly quips, "With my luck, when my ship comes in, I'll be at the bus station or the airport."

In Multi-Level Marketing, you really CAN have your ship come in! If you learn and apply these Napkin presentations, you can be there when it comes in.

I sometimes ask people if they have a long-lost relative that is going to die and leave them a lot of money. The fact is, most people really don't have much of a chance of that happening. Most people really don't have much of a chance for their ship to come in. However, in Multi-Level Marketing, they CAN!

This is just one of the reasons why I am EXCITED about MLM. When you're out talking to people, you can give them HOPE—hope that they don't have to spend the next 30 to 40 years working for a company just so they can draw a pension and retire. Did you ever notice how people work 30 to 40 years so they can retire and "see the world," but then now they are trying to live on half their income?

MULTI-LEVEL MARKETING really does give people the opportunity to see their dreams come true, and they don't have to wait or work 30 or 40 years to see them.

Most people are fearful about trying to start and build a business of their own. MLM gives them the opportunity, without disturbing their present means of support, to get involved and try it out.

What I will show you now is HOW you can have your SHIP COME IN. This would represent your reaching the top of whatever Multi-Level Marketing organization you happen to be involved with.

When your ship arrives, you are going to "cash-in" on whatever cargo it is carrying.

What I do when showing this analogy to someone is to draw three ships at sea. Off to the side or at the bottom of your napkin, you draw the "shore"– that's where you are waiting for your ship to come in.

Label the first ship "GOLD," the second ship "SILVER," and the third ship "M.T." (Empty).

The ships represent the people in your organization, whether you sponsored them directly or not. They may be at any level on down the sponsorship line(s).

Knowing that you were going to "cash-in" on the cargo when your ship comes in, which of the ships are you going to work with to help them reach the shore? The "GOLD" ship you say? Of course! So why is it that most people seem to want to work with the empty ship? Because most people have never been involved in anything like this before.

The parallel is this: The "GOLD" SHIPS are the sales types they've sponsored and left on their own, thinking they don't need any help or direction—they are just going to run with it and really go. Maybe they will–but probably they won't–not without the success keys of building in depth rather than width.

The M.T. ships are the ones that have been in the program several months and you still have to convince them every time you see them that it WILL WORK. They tend to be somewhat negative and easily discouraged.

Most people will work with the empty ship UNTIL they see this presentation. When they understand it, they will start working with the "GOLD" ships.

When you sponsor someone into the business, they come in as a SILVER SHIP. It's basically determined by how YOU work with them whether their cargo turns to GOLD or they remain EMPTY.

When we were talking about your 5 SERIOUS PEOPLE in the first presentation, we were talking about FIVE GOLD SHIPS. Simply put, the more silver ships you have that turn to gold, the fewer you have to sponsor to get your five serious people.

Here is how you can identify a GOLD SHIP or SERIOUS PERSON:

1) They are EAGER to LEARN. They call you all the time with many questions they want answered.

2) They ASK FOR HELP. They have someone they want you to see with them to sponsor or train.

3) They are EXCITED ABOUT THE BUSINESS. They under stand enough about the program to know it will work, and it excites them!

4) They make COMMITMENTS. They are buying and USING THE PRODUCTS, and they are spending their spare time learning all they can about the products and the business opportunity.

5) They have GOALS. Goals help to drive a person to get what they really want. It's not absolutely necessary to have them written down (but it doesn't hurt), just so long as you have some definite things in mind that are a burning desire for you to achieve,

6) They have a LIST OF NAMES. That list WILL be WRITTEN DOWN. The reason for having it written down is simple: you can add to it at any time and you won't forget the name later. You may be driving in an area that you haven't been in for awhile. Just being there will usually jog your memory of someone who lives or used to live in that neighbor- hood. Since you ALWAYS (right?) have your list of names with you, you can immediately add their name to your list. A few days later when you are thinking about calling some one, you can scan down your list, and low and behold, there is that name! If you hadn't written it down when you thought of it, you may have never thought of them again.

7) They are FUN TO BE WITH. They look forward to your coming for a visit, business or pleasure.

8) They are POSITIVE. We all like to be around positive thinking people–it's contagious!

The list could go on and on about the identification of a-gold ship.

Basically, the only difference between a SILVER ship and a GOLD one is the silver hasn't been in the business long enough to understand it to the point of really getting serious about it.

I want you to be aware of THREE IMPOR-TANT WORDS. If you just understand these three words, you would understand what makes all MLM programs work. Those words are:
#1-EXPOSE
#2-INVOLVE
#3-UPGRADE

The first thing you have to do is to EXPOSE the person to the business you are in. Once you have exposed it to them, get them INVOLVED. Once they are involved they will be thinking about how far they can go in the program and will be UPGRADED constantly.

EXPOSE them to Multi-Level Marketing by explaining the various methods (Retail, Direct Sales, MLM) of moving products and show them the "Two Times Two is Four" Napkin Presentation # 1 (Chapter II).

Get them INVOLVED. Take them on a trip to California via Napkin Presentation #3 (Chapter IV).

UPGRADING will be a natural for them once they understand and utilize all ten of the Napkin Presentations and set their sights on the top.

It is very important when you phone or visit your people that they realize you are calling because you WANT TO HELP them, and not because you are PUSHING them.

Referring back to the M.T. (empty) ship type of person: When you call them because you want to help them, you get the feeling that they weren't exactly thrilled about you calling. This is a very good indication that they feel you are being "pushy" and bugging them. When you call "empty ships," they think you are pressuring them.

On the other hand, when you call a gold ship, they just figure that you are calling because you want to help, and you will pick that up in the tone of their conversation.

"Empty ships" don't have goals, they don't have a list of names, they are definitely not serious, and on top of all that they're usually a little bit negative. They are the ones you must keep proving things to all the time.

Realize that when the empty ship sinks, it will either go down alone, or in the event that you work with empty ships rather than gold, it will drag you down with it. That is why I try to train my people to stay away from the empty ships and work with the gold ships, or with the silvers to help them to become gold ships. Spend most of your time working with the gold ships to help them develop their own organizations down-group.

All of a sudden, the M.T.'s who haven't sunk (i.e. dropped from the program), and the silvers who haven't converted to gold yet, will see you moving ahead without them, and they just might call you instead. If a person's attitude about the business is on the way down, trying to stop it enroute is next to impossible. You almost have to let it hit bottom. Then, when they are ready and THEY CALL YOU, and want to get together and get going and get growing, you can bring them up very quickly. But if you run the risk of trying to bring them up while they're on the way down (i.e.-working with a sinking ship, an empty one at that), they very likely could drag you down with them.

This is somewhat of an enjoyable way of communicating with your distributors. When you get together, you can ask them how they are doing with their ships; how many Golds?–how many Silvers?–etc.

An IMPORTANT POINT HERE: NEVER EVER call up a new distributor and ask him HOW MUCH he SOLD last week! If you do, you have totally invalidated everything you've told him, because you told him right up front that he didn't have to go out and SELL. They are just going to SHARE with their friends, SPONSOR, and BUILD an organization.

If you ask them what they've sold, their first reaction will be to think that you are only interested in knowing how much money you are going to make off of them–and they are probably thinking correctly.

The money will come automatically if you seek first to HELP YOUR PEOPLE to SUCCEED. Zig Ziglar puts it this way: "You can have anything in the world that you want, simply by HELPING enough OTHER PEOPLE to get what they want."

When you want to talk to someone in your organization that you sponsored directly, whenever possible, call someone down-line from them and chat with them a little to see if there is anyone you can help them to meet with or talk to. Afterward, you can call the 1st level person you originally wanted to talk to, and the first thing you let them know is that you were just talking with one of their distributors who is excited, and that you are going to get together with them.

Display to your people that when you call, you are calling to HELP them, not to "check-up" on them.

"Checking-up" on their people is the Direct Sales company's Sales Manager's job, not yours. We are not in Direct Sales–we are in Multi-Level Marketing. By now you should be aware of the difference.

To wrap up this presentation, I point out that you, the reader, are NOT an "empty" ship. If you are, you probably wouldn't be reading this book. If you feel you were an M.T. ship before you began to read this book, by the time you get this far you are probably a "gold," or at least a "silver," well on your way to becoming a GOLD SHIP. Keep it up!

# NOTES

# CHAPTER 7
## Napkin Presentation #6
## Third Party Invitation

PROSPECTING is the subject of this presentation, which is actually tied in with the "Ships at Sea" presentation. More simply, we call prospecting the THIRD PARTY INVITATION. It's important that all your people know what a THIRD PARTY INVITATION is and how to do it.

Explanation: If I know Carol, I DON'T go up and ask Carol if she's interested in earning some extra income. The reason I don't do that is because even if Carol wanted (or even needed) to earn some extra money, she would probably want me to think that she's doing okay financially and she would say, "No, I'm really not interested."

What I can DO, is go up to Carol and say something like, "Carol, I got started in a new exciting business, and you might be able to help me. Would you happen to KNOW ANYONE who would be interested in earning some extra income?" (or, "Interested in getting into a second business?")

Notice the "Third Party"–ANYONE. I'm asking her if she KNOWS ANYONE.

Do a little experimenting on this. The next ten people you run into, (gas station attendant, grocer, barber, cleaners, etc.), ask them if they KNOW ANYBODY who'd like to earn some extra income; just to get their reaction. Their response will tell you something.

Most of the time their response will probably be, "What is it?" The reason they say, "What is it?" is because the person THEY KNOW who would like to earn some extra income is THEMSELVES–they just want to know a little more about it so they can make a decision.

When they say "What is it?", don't give them the big curiosity shot. Some people are offended by getting dragged off to somebody's home for an hour-and-a-half presentation and they have no idea why they are going there. (Some companies train their people to not say anything.) Your reply when they ask you what it is will be, "Do you know anything about Multi-Level Marketing?" They will either say "Yes" or "No." If they say "Yes", ask them what they know about it. Get into a GENERAL DISCUSSION with them about MLM. (Refer to Chapter I–"Introduction to MLM") Point out some of the features and benefits of being involved in Multi-Level Marketing in general.

From there, invite them to sit down with you (if they're still interested) to take a look at the PARTICULAR PROGRAM that you're in. Explain to them that it would take only an hour or so to tell them the WHOLE STORY. Don't try to "shotgun" the program to them on a street corner or while they are supposed to be working. Without the WHOLE STORY you'd just be confusing them. Just enough confusing information for them to say "No", and not enough information for them to say "Yes."

If you follow the training of your people the way it's laid out for you, you won't have to prospect. In the process of helping the people that you brought into the business, you will run into other people that you will be able to talk to. When you run into these people, you want to talk to them about Multi-Level Marketing so you can introduce them to your program. Most people have some fears about doing that. Where those fears come from is the idea that the person will say "No" to them. It's called the "FEAR OF REJECTION."

A good example would be at a high school dance. A guy is at the first dance he's ever been to. He walks clear across the room and asks a girl to dance, and she says "No." So he turns around, REJECTED, and walks back, never again to ask a girl to dance. He will absolutely swear that everybody in the whole auditorium SAW him get rejected. Nobody likes to be rejected.

Another type will ask a girl to dance, and if she says "No" he will ask the next girl and the next ... and that fellow will be dancing all night.

To OVERCOME the fear of rejection, I want you to be able to trick your mind so you will be able to talk to more people. To do that, picture yourself standing on a dock. Remember, if you are waiting for YOUR ship to come in, you'll have had to already have sent your ship(s) out.

You have to LAUNCH some ships. If you launched only one ship and it returned empty, what good did it do to have your ship "come-in" at all? The more ships you launch, the better chance you will have of some of them coming in carrying GOLD. The ships carrying GOLD are the ones you should work with.

Most people have never launched a ship, so there's nothing already in your sub-conscious that can hurt you. Notice the launching ramp. When you ask someone if they KNOW ANYBODY who would like to earn some extra income, you have just launched a ship. If they say, "No, I don't know anybody," you can say, "Fine. If you happen to run into anybody, would you have them call me?" (Give them your card.) So you weren't rejected.

There are only two possible results in launching a ship. It will either FLOAT, or it will SINK.

If it SINKS, so what! You're standing on the dock!

If it FLOATS, Great! Send it out and help it to turn into a gold-carrying vessel.

After presenting the Napkin Presentations #5 and #6, people will tell you they plan on being a "gold." The reason they tell you that is because you have just told them that you only work with the GOLD SHIPS, and they WANT YOU TO WORK WITH THEM. Take advantage of their invitation—you will benefit also!

# NOTES

# NOTES

# CHAPTER 8
## Napkin Presentation #7
## Where To Spend Your Time

BELOW IS A GRAPH which lays out pictorially where you should be spending your time. Basically, 100% of your time at the beginning should be spent sponsoring people.

"But," you ask, "should I not be spending my time training, as the first few weeks are supposed to be my TRAINING MONTH?" You are correct. But remember, your sponsor helping you to sponsor, IS part of your training. Even though your sponsor does the "work," YOU still get credit for being the sponsor.

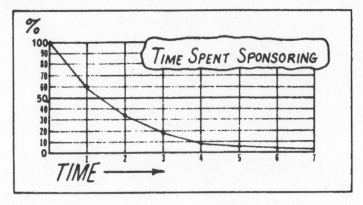

In MLM programs you can sponsor someone else into the business just as soon as you have been sponsored.

When you first get into MLM, your business is YOU. If you want your business to be successful, you now know that you must find 5 SERIOUS PEOPLE to sponsor. You may have to sponsor more than 5 to find 5 that want to be serious.

As time goes on, the amount of time you spend on sponsoring people, drops off. Why? Because all of a sudden you find one serious person... then two serious people...then three...four...and when you have five serious people, you can quit spending your time looking for people to sponsor. Spend your time TEACHING those 5 "Gold Ships" to sponsor. Teach them also to teach their people to sponsor. When they have gone 3 or 4 deep in building their own groups and don't need you any more, then you can go looking for another serious person to sponsor to replace them.

When you have five serious people, you should be spending 95 % of your time working with them, 2 1/2% of your time servicing the customers you have from your friends, and 2 1/2% of your time "planting seeds." This way, when one or more of your 5 serious people are "harvested," and don't need to be "watered and cultivated" any more, you can work with the "seeds" you planted and help them to "sprout."

You should be aware that 100% of the time, you are moving the product. It's a natural result of working with your people. That's the "selling" part of the business, which I like to call the "SHARING" part.

# NOTES

# NOTES

# CHAPTER 9
## Napkin Presentation #8
## The Sizzle Sells The Steak

ANOTHER TITLE that I sometimes use for this presentation is "The Blazes." I assume you have been camping. You will notice that if you separate the logs of a campfire, the fire will go out. If you put them back together again, the fire will blaze up. So if you have ONE LOG you have NOTHING.

If you have TWO LOGS, you'll have a FLAME. When you put THREE LOGS together, you will have a FIRE.

By the time you put together FOUR LOGS, you'll have a BLAZE!!

People are the same way. The next time you're meeting someone with your sponsor, in a restaurant for example, and arriving first (being there by yourself), notice how much ENERGY there is (or ISN'T) around the table.

Notice that when your sponsor arrives and there are two of you, how there is MUCH MORE ENERGY!

The two of you are there to meet with someone, and when they arrive, there is EVEN MORE ENERGY.

When the fourth person arrives, you've really got it going! We like to call these "blazes" or "SIZZLE SESSIONS." Your MLM program is the "steak," and everybody knows—The SIZZLE sells the Steak!

So you want to get together with your sponsor and share the Napkin Presentations with one or two of your down-line people. Get them "Sizzling" and excited about what can happen.

A good place to do this is in a restaurant. Pick a time when the restaurant is the least busy, around 10 a.m. or 2 p.m. You may want to set up a schedule so your people will know where you'll be at various times during the week. It's as if everybody's out gathering wood for the fire or BLAZE.

If you were to bring someone to a "Sizzle Session" who is a little bit skeptical (a "wet log") and introduce them to the BLAZE, they would dry out and become part of the fire.

So what happens if you are all by yourself and you, being new in the business, talk to someone who is skeptical? That's like trying to put a wet log on nothing.

Let's say you are a twig, just getting started in the business. Your sponsor, who's been around a little longer, is a LOG. A LOG and a TWIG can create a FLAME. Just having someone with you can make a difference. It gives your sponsor someone to bounce conversation off. I could want Joe to get a message, and if I'm talking to him directly, he might not really "hear" what I'm saying. But if I'm talking to Carol, knowing that Joe is listening…it's amazing how people get more out of conversations they "listen-in" to than if someone was talking to them directly.

Another thing about these BLAZES in a restaurant: they get very energetic! There are people (called "eavesdroppers") who could be "listening-in" on some of the conversation. You can spot them, leaning back, trying to hear more…etc. BE AWARE, some of these people will be VERY interested. When you're all done with your Sizzle Session and start to break up, STICK AROUND a few more minutes. Give them an opportunity to approach you. They won't come over to the table when there are four people there, but they may come over if you are by yourself.

I always start the "blazing" sessions by having the people, as they arrive, tell something positive that has happened with the products or their organization. While we're there we talk only about the business. We don't try to solve the Middle-East crisis or any of the world's other problems. WE are there to share ideas about how to build our business and how to talk to people about our business.

We always break up our sessions with a parting word that goes something like, "Just think! This is as hard as we will ever work!" This gets a little contagious, especially if you have people join your group who still have their regular 9-to-5 job and have to leave because their "lunch hour" is gone. You might say to them as they leave to go back to work, "See you later Nick, but remember..." He may interrupt with, "Yeah, I know. That's as hard as you'll ever work." Nick will be motivated to hurry up and get to that same position.

# NOTES

# CHAPTER 10
## Napkin Presentation #9
## Motivation And Attitude

ONE OF THE MOST IMPORTANT of the Napkin presentations is this one on MOTIVATION. This will give you an excellent understanding of what motivates people. You will learn how to work with your people to motivate them.

Start out by writing the word "MOTIVA-TION" at the top of your napkin or board. Next draw two arrows-one pointing down, and the other pointing up. Point out that there are two kinds of motivation: DOWN MO-TIVATION and UP MOTIVATION. Label the arrows. DOWN MOTIVATION is what

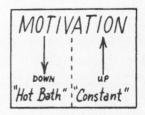

we call "hot bath" but UP MOTIVATION is "constant". Let me explain. Most of you probably have been to rah-rah motivational rallies and found yourself gung-ho to get with it and get going (again) with the program you are in. You usually find that you've cooled off again in a couple of weeks or months. When you take a hot bath, it seems the hotter the bath, the quicker you seem to cool off.

I have seen people go to motivational rallies that last up to three days–then two weeks after they get home, they are totally depressed. Why? For three days they get hyped up, really motivated-but nobody told them WHAT to do and/or HOW to do it! That's why they get down.

Even reading this book is "hot bath." (I'll get to UP motivation in a lit-tle bit.) Going to seminars, getting together with your sponsor, reading a book, moving some product, obtaining more knowledge–these are all

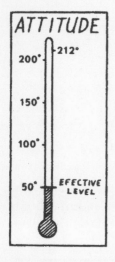

forms of "hot bath" or down-motivation. That's not to say they are bad, for they are necessary.

Before I talk about UP MOTIVATION, I want to talk about attitude. Imagine that you are going to talk to someone about your business. That person doesn't know anything about it, so they have an attitude level of zero. Let's say for you to be effective in talking to them about the business, you need an attitude level of 50 degrees. If your attitude level is short of 50 degrees, don't talk to anybody, because they will just drag you down.

Suppose the person you want to sponsor has come to your presentation. They have signed the application. They want to get started—and boy are they excited about the business! They're all the way up to 65 degrees—they're going to get RICH! Before they have had a chance to learn anything, they go out and start talking to people. Since they really don't know how to handle themselves when confronted by negative skeptics, they get negative themselves, even from well-meaning relatives and friends who may have been disillusioned by getting "signed up" by someone who just wanted to "get rich" off them, rather than by someone who was willing or able to help them build a business, a real "sponsor", with a commitment to helping others ahead of helping himself or herself.

What will happen is they will drop below the 50 degree level. You get back together with them again, answer their objections and questions they may have, and they'll go back up, maybe to 70 degrees. And this time they will stay up a little bit longer before they go below 50 degrees again in their attitude level.

THE QUESTION: How would you like to have an attitude level about 50 degrees ALL THE TIME? In other words, you aren't up and down like a YO-YO, but you want to be CONSTANT. The only way I know of that you can do that is with UP MOTIVATION—because UP MOTIVATION is CONSTANT.

Here is UP MOTIVATION: You have a sponsor. Your sponsor (SP.) will help to sponsor people FOR YOU. We start with 5. Notice that when you sponsor 5 people, you have only 25 degrees. Again, a mistake to avoid: sponsoring more than you can effectively work with, adding 5 degrees at a time and losing them just as fast.

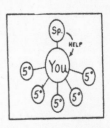

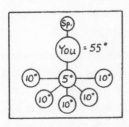

Your sponsor helped you sponsor these 5 people, and you in turn will help those 5 people sponsor others for their 5 degrees. Their 5 degrees is 10 degrees for you. All the second level people are worth 10 degrees each for you. NOTICE: if you only helped one of the 5 people to sponsor 5 others, that would put you above 50 degrees.

Notice what happens when you teach sponsoring down another level. The third level is 20 degrees. The fourth is 40 degrees. The deeper you go the hotter it gets!

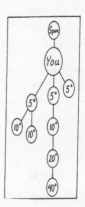

The only way you can appreciate this phenomenon is when it's first happening–and that's why you want it to happen to your people as soon as it can possibly happen for them. Once they experience it they will be EXCITED!

Here is an example: Carol sponsors Tom, and Tom sponsors Bill. Carol gets a phone call and finds out that Bill went out last week and sponsored 5 serious people–

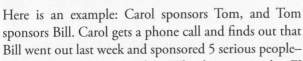

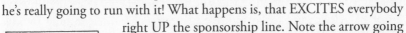

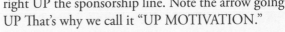

he's really going to run with it! What happens is, that EXCITES everybody right UP the sponsorship line. Note the arrow going UP That's why we call it "UP MOTIVATION."

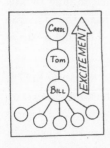

You need to help the people you sponsored to SUPPORT their people. Let me show you an exception to that. When you sponsor someone into the business, they are a Silver Ship. Everyone comes in as a Silver. They're excited, but they haven't gotten serious yet.

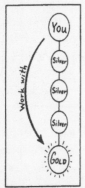

Everybody has at least one friend. Get together with your people. Help them to sponsor some of their friends who come in as Silver Ships. SUPPORT your people as they help their friends to sponsor more friends on down-line 3 or more deep. All of a sudden, down line there somewhere, you will find someone who turns out to be a GOLD SHIP. Here is what you do: Go down and work with that first real GOLD you have in that line. What will happen is, that in the process of helping the Gold, the Silvers will be converted to Gold.

That is how you convert the Silvers; get someone under them. If that person under them really goes (is a Gold) the Silver that had sponsored them will say, "Hey! I'd better get my act together . . ." There isn't anything that will motivate people more, than to have someone under them DOING SOMETHING. It has been said, "You can motivate people faster and more effectively by putting a candle under their sitting place than by putting a blow-torch to their thinking place."

To wrap this up: the one thing you don't want to do is have the people you have sponsored develop a dependency on you. The people you sponsor cannot be dependent on you forever; otherwise, it's not going to work. There has got to be a point where they don't need you. We say this point is when your people can teach their people to teach all ten of the Napkin Presentations–then they know everything they need to know to build a strong organization. Then you can go find another serious person to replace them.

Let's suppose for this example that you sponsored Sue. You would say, "Sue, let's say you are like the sun. The sun has more energy than anything we know of" (It is kind of an indirect compliment.) You continue by saying, "The person you (Sue) sponsor is like a pan of water." (NOTE: You sponsored Sue, but don't assume the role of the sun and call her a pan of water–it's not that flattering.)

So, in your group there is a "sun." At what point would the water boil? If you took a pan of water and set it out in the middle of the hottest desert on the hottest day of the year, it still would not boil. It will take 212 degrees for the water to begin to boil. It won't boil at 210 degrees or 211 degrees, it has to be at least 212 degrees to boil.

So notice: if your attitude is at 212 degrees, and only needs to be at 50 degrees to be effective, you could talk to anybody at anytime about what you're doing. So that's the direction your attitude is heading. We just told you that the sun can't make the water boil. Your sponsor can't make the water boil either. None of the "hot bath" motivation can.

I don't care if all the top people in all of the Multi-Level companies came to town for a rally and you went to all of them–your water will never boil. They can get your attitude above the 50 degree effective level, but it's up to you to get the water boiling. And remember, your sponsor will help you.

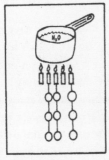

In other words, you know some people your sponsor doesn't know. Your sponsor will go with you and help you sponsor someone. Once you have sponsored someone, you have started the burner under the pan. With five people sponsored, you now have the pan sitting on 5 jets of the burner, the maximum number the pan can effectively cover. Notice the water isn't boiling yet; it's only 25 degrees if your five people have not sponsored anyone yet. But, if any three run off a string three deep, or any two a string four deep, or any one a string five deep, the water begins to boil.

Any combination that adds up to 212 under the pan will get the water to boil. At the time the water is boiling, the sun (sponsor) can go away and the water will continue to boil. Once you've shown a person this and you call them on the phone, they realize that you are calling because you want to help them. You are not calling to give them a blow-torch to the head, but rather you are calling to see if you can light another burner or turn the temperature up on those already lit. You want to help them get their water to boil. The farther you go down the group, the hotter the burner gets.

In all the programs, once you have a person with their water boiling, it may look similar to the example on the left. Notice that you have others sponsored as well. The first one to boil is not necessarily the first one you sponsored. It is the first one that got serious and got the depth in their organization to get, and keep, it going.

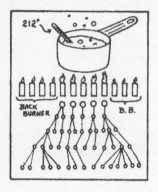

When the water boils there, you can continue working with 5 serious people. Notice that the pan can sit on only 5 burners at a time. (This kind of goes along with the first presentation in Chapter II.) If you have 15 people sponsored into the business, you can really work effectively with only 5 at a time. You may have to sponsor 10 to 20 people to get those 5 serious people. What happens to the others? We put them on the back burner so to speak.

So, when you have the water boiling on one or more of the "5," before you go out to search for someone brand new to sponsor, take a trip around to the back burner and let them know what's going on. You may find that because of timing and circumstances, at the time you sponsored them, they weren't ready yet to get serious about the business, but they are ready now. Maybe they were just waiting to see how the program was going to work for you. So take a trip around to the back burner.

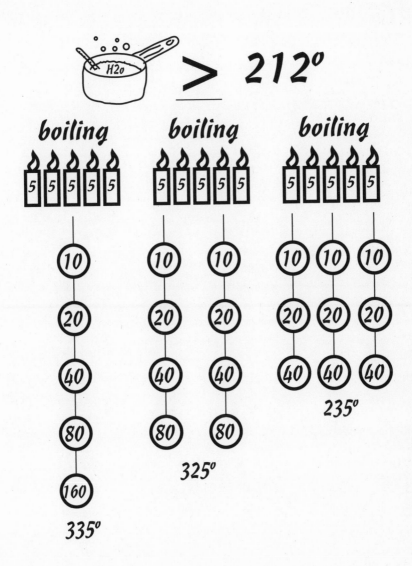

# NOTES

# CHAPTER 11
## Napkin Presentation #10
## Pentagon Of Growth

FIVE has been the "magic" number throughout this book, so it's only appropriate that this final presentation is a 5-sided fun trip of a mathematical exercise, which also tends toward being a SELF-MOTIVATOR every time you show it to someone.

This "Pentagon of Growth" lays out an important view of how FAST your organization can grow, if you adopt the principles which we have outlined in this book.

Start by drawing a pentagon and writing "YOU" in the middle of it. We'll allow for a Training Month and use increments of two months as we develop our organization. (You can use whatever time frame you wish, however.)

You come into the business and in two months you have sponsored five people who really want to get a handle on life. (Write 2M-5 by one side of the pentagon as shown in the figure for "2 Months.")

In 2 more months (i.e. at the end of four months), the five from the second month having been taught to do what you're doing, give you 25 second-level distributors. At the same time you have developed 5

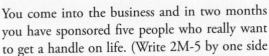

more serious first level people. Your pentagon is now looking like the one above.

After 6 months you may have 125 third-level people under your "original" five, 25 second-levels under your second group of five serious people, plus you have developed a third set of five.

At the end of 8 months: your pentagon of growth may appear like the example to the left.

Now at this point, hand the napkin (or board) over to your student, give them the pen, and have them complete the diagram on out for 10 months. Just put a line for 10 months (10M ___ ) of the original group, as the figure is too large to effectively identify with, as it's over 3,000. (3,125 to be exact.) The example to the right is what they should now have.

Go around the pentagon one more time and extend it to a year.

To really put emphasis on how building in depth can make your organization grow rapidly, cross out all of the groups-except the one under your original five serious people. Point out to the person you are showing this

to, that if all they built was this one group (and they didn't do any of the ones crossed out), they would be making $6,000 per MONTH or more-depending on the "vehicle" they were using. The main purpose of this exercise is to simply show the importance of working DOWN-GROUP with the people that you sponsor–and TEACHING THEM TO DO THE SAME.

Now Go Do It!

# NOTES

# NOTES

# CHAPTER 12
## Going Back To School

YOUR ATTITUDE can make a big difference when you are trying to sponsor a new distributor. Most distributors seem to have the attitude, "Who can I get into my business?" I think the proper attitude is "To whom will I next offer the opportunity to retire?" If you believe a person could retire in one to three years and you understood how to present this possibility in a presentation that takes only two minutes, why would you want to give this opportunity to a stranger?

To be able to retire in one to three years at better than $50,000 per year a person must be willing to go back to school. They can learn everything they would need to know by investigating five to ten hours per week for six months. "Retiring" simply means: "...not going to work unless you want to." If someone tells you they will give it thirty days to see how it goes, don't waste your time. You can't dig your foundation in thirty days. It takes at least six months.

The school I am referring to is a school of INVOLVEMENT. From the time you leave your home for your weekly training session, attend the meeting, have coffee and drive home, you have already spent three to five hours. The rest of the time is spent listening to positive motivation tapes, tapes about your program, meeting with your sponsor, attending sizzle sessions, talking to prospects, etc. This can all be done along with anything else you have already been doing outside of MLM.

While doing seminars across the world, I have asked this question, "Does anyone know of a four-year college course where you could graduate, then hope to retire in one to three years at better than $50,000 per year?" I have never had anyone tell me of one. No one anywhere can come up with a college course where that is even a remote possibility. That is what is exciting about MLM. You can actually learn in six months everything you need to know to retire in one to three years.

Do you remember when you were in college and you went to the bookstore and bought your books for the quarter? Big, heavy, thick text books. You could hardly wait to get back to your room so you could start studying them. Do you remember how you could hardly wait until the end of the quarter to be tested on the material? While you were going to school, did anyone pay you for going? Since you went to college for four years without getting paid and since you had no hope of retiring in one to three years, then why do you get so concerned about how little you have made in your first few months in MLM? Remember, you are in school. MLM school.

Some people in MLM get discouraged after only a few weeks. I don't think they have a right to be discouraged unless they have had at least six months of MLM school. Try letting a medical student operate on you after they have been in school for a few weeks. You would probably be very disappointed with the outcome.

Ask a doctor, a lawyer, a dentist, or any other professional person how long they have been practicing their profession. Their answer will be figured from the time they graduated, not from their first day as a college freshman. When you ask someone in MLM how long they have been in the business, they will tell you from the day they first signed their Distributor Agreement or Application. You should actually keep track of the time you are in the MLM business beginning from the time when you knew what you were doing.

The only time you will be disappointed is when you expect something and you don't get it or it doesn't happen. Too many distributors come into MLM expecting to start making big money right away. First and foremost you need to go to school. That will take at least six months. Consider those going to college. After six months into their freshman year they still have three and a half years to go before they are even ready to look for a job.

To be really successful in MLM you must teach someone else to be successful. Your distributors need to quit being so concerned about what kind of money they are making and increase their concern for teaching and working with their downline. The quicker they do this, the quicker they will find real success in MLM. But this takes time. Before you can teach others, you first must learn what to do yourself.

If you have distributors in your organization who have trouble talking to their friends, it's probably because they really don't believe they could retire in one to three years, or they don't understand how they could actually make it happen. The following is a simple presentation you can use to show how someone could build a large income in six months to three years. It only takes a few minutes to learn and about two minutes to make a presentation. It is a variation taken from Napkin Presentation #1 in Chapter II.

Let's assume that you have a new distributor to whom you say, "With all of the people you know or could meet with my help, do you think you could sponsor five persons by the end of your first month? People who would like to learn how to retire in one to three years?"

Most people will say, "Everyone I know would like to be able to do that."

Don't make the mistake of going with your distributor to see five people at one time. Go with your distributor five times to see each person individually. If you see all five, at once, one negative person could spoil it for the other four. Besides, if you go with your distributor five times your distributor will get to see the presentation five times rather than only once. Now with this training they will be ready to go with each of their distributors five times. Your distributor will become an expert practicing on their distributor's prospects, just as you have become an expert practicing on their prospects.

If you can sponsor five SERIOUS distributors by the end of your first thirty days you should be able to help them sponsor five by the end of three months. When your distributors are helping their five, you are now supporting down group and teaching your people to do the same. You should be at the third level by the end of six months. So what if it took a year? When making this presentation, the lines (-5-) on either side of the 5, 25, and 125 represent your wholesale buyers or the people who signed up to get you off their back. Your presentation should look like this:

At this point you would have a total of 155 SERIOUS distributors.

If you are building your business right, in the process of sharing your opportunity, you will have some who will not take advantage of it. Many of these will become either a wholesale buyer or a retail customer.

Let us say that each of your distributors down line has at least ten friend-customers. When you multiply ten friend-customers by 155 serious distributors, you would have 1,550 friend-customers. Since your distributors are also customers, you need to add 155 to 1,550 giving you a total customer count of 1,705. Also consider, there are three reasons why a distributor-customer will purchase more products than a friend-customer: 1) The distributor-customer is more familiar with the entire line of products; 2) The distributor-customer can buy the products wholesale and is more likely to be generous with their use personally; 3) The distributor-customer buys products to give away as samples. You should encourage all of your distributors to use samples as well as using samples yourself.

The line under the "155" represents your wholesale buyers which we are not counting. This would only mean a plus. Your presentation at this point would look something like this:

Now multiply the 1,705 times $30 to get total group sales per month.

Most of you are in programs where your personal sales are much more than $30 per month. I use this figure to be a little conservative. You don't want to completely blow your prospect's mind. That is why at level 3 you ask. "What if it took a year instead of six months? Would it be worth it?"

```
                    — You —      155 Serious Distrib.
End of 1ˢᵀ Mo. — 5 —        x 10 Friend Customers
End of 3ʳᵈ Mo. — 25 —      ―――――――
End of 6ᵗʰ Mo. — 125 —     1550  "        "
                          + 155 Distrib.  "
                          ----- Wholesale Buyers
                          ――――――
                          1705 Total Customers
```

When you multiply $30 times 1,705 total customers, you come up with $51,150 total volume. Point out that you are only working with just FIVE SERIOUS distributors.

With a volume of over $50,000 per month in sales, not counting your wholesale buyers, you should be making somewhere between $2,000 and $6,000 per month.

The reason for the spread between $2,000 and $6,000 per month is everyone may not have their ten friend-customers; some may have more.

At this point, you should be into your presentation 10 to 15 minutes. This is when you ask the question that lets you know if your prospect is willing to take the time to learn how to drive. If they say "no," go right to the products and get another retail customer. If they say "yes," go to the next presentation, the difference between 5 and 6. When you complete this presentation they will be more than ready to check out your vehicle.

**Here is the $64 question. If you could be making $2,000 to $6,000 per month in six months on top of what you are currently earning, could you see yourself going back to school for five to ten hours per week for six months to learn how to do it?**

This presentation is simple, and it explains the mechanics of how an organization can grow. It is a combination of building the organization and everyone retailing a minimum amount. Anyone can build ten friend-customers. It doesn't take a salesperson to do this. When completed, you entire presentation should look like this:

The meaning of a SERIOUS distributor in this presentation is a distributor who has made the following commitment: They will get involved for a minimum of five to ten hours per week for at least six months. This is the only way they can learn the business.

```
                    —You—          155 Serious Distrib.
        End of 1ˢᵗ Mo. —5—        x 10 Friend Customers
                                   ─────
        End of 3ʳᵈ Mo. —25—        1550    "        "
        End of 6ᵗʰ Mo. —125—      + 155 Distrib.   "
            (or Year)             ----- Wholesale Buyers
                                   ─────
                                   1705 Total Customers
                                   x $30

                                  $51,150 Total Volume
```

# NOTES

# NOTES

# CHAPTER 13
## Playing With Numbers
## To Make A Point

SO WHAT do you do when one of your front liners (personally sponsored distributors) reaches the point where they don't need you anymore? (Refer to Napkin Presentation #9, Chapter X.) You are now free to sponsor someone else and work a new line. The definition of a "line" is when your distributor's organization is at least three levels deep.

Instead of wondering who you are going to bring into your business, you now get to make a choice. Out of all the people you have met while working down group with your first five SERIOUS distributors, you now get to select one who will have an opportunity for early retirement.

It is exciting to realize that you can select someone who will get this opportunity. You carry a lot of power when you totally understand and believe.

Now you have six serious distributors in your front line. Point out the difference between five and six which is of course, one. Continue downgroup. Six times six equals 36. Five times five equals 25. The difference between 36 and 25 is 11. Do it one more time. Five times 25 is 125. Six times 36 is 216 and the difference between 216 and 125 is 91. Your presentation at this point should now look something like this:

| You | Difference | You |
|-----|-----------|-----|
| 5 | 1 | 6 |
| 25 | 11 | 36 |
| 125 | 91 | 216 |

All programs that have breakaways will pay well beyond five levels and most unilevel programs will pay down seven levels. Continue down-line with the multiples of five to the seventh level. Your presentation should now look like this:

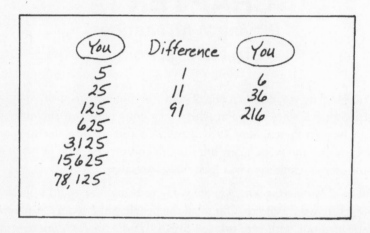

This presentation is easy to learn. Notice that when you get to 125 in the level column the last 3 digits alternate between 125 and 625. This would continue no matter how many levels you go down. So all you have to remember is 3, 15, 78.

At this point in the presentation you suggest to your distributor that he or she complete the calculations on their own. In other words, multiply 216 times 6 (which is 1,296) and subtract 625 from it. That is a difference of 671. Continue this process down to the seventh level. The impact will be much greater if you have them do it themselves.

Ask this question: "What do you think the answer will be at the seventh level?" Let them guess. Most of them will not even come close. The difference at the seventh level is over 200,000! 201,811 to be precise. Your presentation should now look like the diagram on page 79.

Obviously, 201,811 is quite a difference. You should mention to your distributor that once someone understands this they can see the importance of working down-group. Why be concerned with having so many in your

| You | Difference | You |
|-----|-----------|-----|
| 5 | 1 | 6 |
| 25 | 11 | 36 |
| 125 | 91 | 216 |
| 625 | ? | — |
| 3,125 | ? | — |
| 15,625 | ? | — |
| 78,125 | 201,811 | — |

front line? You couldn't work with them anyway. Besides, sponsoring too many in your front line gets you involved in a game we call "adding and subtracting." I would much rather play the game of multiplication called Multi-Level Marketing or MLM for short.

All you have to do to play this game is teach your people three deep. When you teach three deep you will actually end up five deep. For example: My name is Don and I sponsor Steve. I say to Steve, "When getting a new person started, the most important thing you can teach them is to make sure when they sponsor someone to get them three deep as soon as possible."

Before they even know about it, this will automatically bring Napkin Presentation #9 on motivation into play.

Steve is a good student. When he sponsors Pam, he helps her and supports her down-line making sure she works three deep. This is a variation from Napkin Presentation #2 and should look like the diagram on page 80.

Now count the depth. You have five levels below you. You taught Steve to make sure his people are three deep. Steve will now teach his people what you taught him and you will go even deeper. Can you see now why teachers do so well in MLM?

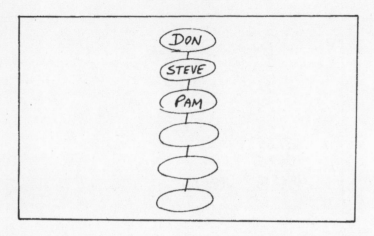

Most "salesmen," when they get started building an organization, think it is a sponsor, sponsor and sponsor business. Actually, what it is, is a sponsor and teach, sponsor and teach, sponsor and teach business. You will never make it in MLM until you teach someone else how to make it.

If you continue your presentation showing the difference between five and six to the fourth level, you would have 1,296 minus 625 for a difference of 671. The total of the differences through the first four levels would be 774. Your total distributors on the left side would be 780 and the total on the right side would be 1,554. Your presentation would now look like this:

| You | Difference | You |
|---|---|---|
| 5 | 1 | 6 |
| 25 | 11 | 36 |
| 125 | 91 | 216 |
| 625 | 671 | 1296 |
| Totals 780 | 774 | 1554 |

You are now on your own. Multiply 780 or 1,554 times 10 friend-customers. Add the friend-customers to the distributor-customers. Now multiply this total by $30 per month and then multiply the result times twelve months. Remember, I am not even considering the wholesale buyers. Now can you see how one could retire in one to three years? You can't do it sponsoring wide without going deep.

This presentation is a continuation of Napkin presentation #1.

$$
\begin{array}{ll}
\begin{array}{r} 780 \\ \times 10 \\ \hline 7800 \\ + 780 \\ \hline 8{,}580 \\ \times \$30 \\ \hline \$257{,}400/\text{mo} \\ \times \quad 12 \\ \hline \$3{,}088{,}800/\text{yr.} \end{array}
&
\begin{array}{r} 1{,}554 \\ \times 10 \\ \hline 15{,}540 \\ + 1{,}554 \\ \hline 17{,}094 \\ \times \$30 \\ \hline \$512{,}820/\text{mo} \\ \times \quad 12 \\ \hline \$6{,}153{,}840/\text{yr.} \end{array}
\end{array}
$$

Friend Customers

Distributor Customers

Months

# NOTES

# CHAPTER 14
## Business Training Sessions Vs. Weekly Opportunity Meetings

MOST PEOPLE in MLM get their start by attending a weekly opportunity meeting. Since this is how they came into the business, they think that weekly opportunity meetings and getting people to them is what the business is all about. After they have invited so many to the meeting, they quit inviting. This is because they figure they have more than enough coming. What happens? On the night of the meeting no one shows up. This can be very discouraging.

A typical opportunity meeting will look something like this: A room is set up with chairs in theatre style, either in a home or a hotel room. A blackboard or whiteboard is sitting on an easel up front. A person in a three-piece suit is giving a presentation about the company, the products, and of course, the marketing plan. This, in most cases, lasts for approximately one and one-half hours.

Out of 22 people who show up for the opportunity meeting there will be 19 distributors and three new guests. Most of those invited as guests didn't even show up. The person putting on the meeting is talking to the guests. He or she is talking to only three of the 22 people there! For the distributor who has already been to the meeting several times and seen the same presentation over and over, this becomes very boring. One tends to get what I call "meeting burn-out."

During the presentation you keep an eye on the guests and you notice positive nods when the speaker is talking about the company, the products, and marketing plan. With all this positive body language, why do your guests sometimes turn down the opportunity when asked if they see themselves getting started? It doesn't make any sense that they could like everything they have seen and heard and still say, "No."

The reason for the "No" is simple. They look at the person putting on the presentation as being "successful." They think that for themselves to be successful they will have to put on meetings. Maybe not right away, but some-time they will have to put on meetings—a thing most people fear even more than the fear of dying. They fear getting up in front of a group of people and speaking. Now you can understand why they turn down the opportunity you have offered. (By the way, that's an important point: They have said "No" to the opportunity, not to you personally. Don't let these "No's" discourage you.)

I prove this point while I'm doing seminars. I say, "Since I'm limited for time, I only have time to call on one person. Would the people who would like to come up and talk about anything they choose for the next three minutes, please raise your hand." Very few, less than 5%, raise their hand. You should see the look of relief on the faces of those who did when I tell them I was only kidding.

I know hundreds of people who can carry on a conversation with a friend over a cup of coffee. These same people freak out at even the thought of getting up in front of a group. Even the size of the group doesn't make any difference. Some company presidents even break out in a cold sweat when merely getting up in front of their board of directors or making a presentation to the stockholders.

How would you like to avoid this fear when building your organization? How would you like to have exciting weekly opportunity meetings? You can. Once you understand HOW, your organization will grow many times faster.

I meet with my prospects one-on-one or at a "Sizzle Session." (See Chapter IX, Napkin Presentation #8). I prefer to meet in a restaurant at an off time for the restaurant. I invite my guest to bring a tape recorder. They could use the tape to review the presentation later or as a tool to help them sponsor their friends.

I always prefer that they have read this book, prior to my meeting with them. This can save you a considerable amount of time. If they already know "how to drive" before you meet with them, it's easier to help them select a "vehicle." (Refer to Napkin Presentation #3 in chapter IV.)

After some idle conversation about the benefits of MLM, tell them you would like to give them a twenty-minute presentation about your company, products and marketing plan. Since you announced that it only takes about twenty minutes, it points out that anyone could learn to give a twenty-minute presentation. Besides, until they learn it, all they have to do is play the tape for their friends.

If it takes you an hour and one-half to present your company, products, and marketing plan, you may become too selective about who you are making appointments with. How many one and one-half hour appointments are you up to doing? When you get your presentation down to twenty minutes you can be productive during a coffee break or make a couple of presentations during your lunch break.

I would break the twenty-minute presentation down as follows: 3 minutes to talk about the company and seven minutes to talk about the products and give them some samples. Allow about ten minutes to explain the marketing plan. Break your total marketing plan into several parts. In most cases you will not need to explain the latter parts to get your person started. Remember, they have made a commitment to go back to school for five to ten hours a week to learn the business. During your first meeting don't try to show them everything they will learn in the next six months.

The two most important words in MLM are SPONSOR and TEACH. The least important word is "sell." "Sell" should always be replaced with the word "share." The next three words of importance are EXPOSE, INVOLVE, and UPGRADE. First you EXPOSE a person to your business.

Then you get them INVOLVED for five to ten hours per week over the next six months. Their knowledge and motivation as to where they want to go in the business will UPGRADE as they go along. They may come in thinking about making an additional $300 to $500 per month, but after being involved for six months their thinking will probably be upgraded to making several thousand dollars on a monthly basis.

If your prospect forgets his tape recorder, bring yours and let them keep the tape when you are finished. When you start your twenty-minute presentation, ask them to write down any questions they may have and explain that you will answer them when you are finished. Point out that if you had to answer questions during the presentation, you wouldn't be able to keep it to twenty minutes.

The tool (the tape) you are giving your new distributor gives you a valid reason for keeping your presentation orderly, without interruption every two minutes. The tape presentation will also be orderly. If you were to answer one question during your presentation, it would be like trying to let only one of several cats out of a bag. Once you start jumping around you will lose the continuity of your presentation.

If your prospect shows any hesitation as to whether they could do the business, simply say to them, "Before you make your final decision, why don't you come to our weekly training session and see how we train our people?"

The purpose of the weekly training session is to teach your distributors how to sit down with a friend over a cup of coffee and give a twenty-minute presentation about your company, products, and marketing plan. The entire training session should not last more than one hour.

Unlike an opportunity meeting, in a weekly training session you are directing your conversation toward your distributors rather than toward the guests. Have you ever noticed how much more believable a conversation is when you are listening in on it rather than having it directed to you? While you are teaching your distributors how to present your company, products, and marketing plan, your guests are getting trained also.

The net result of this style of teaching is that you now have 19 distributors who are better prepared to share the opportunity and three guests who get involved because they can visualize themselves doing the business. One person can be the trainer for the entire city, so you never project the idea that a person would have to get up in front of a group to be successful.

It is very important to get your distributors together at least once a week. Remember Napkin Presentation #8 on Sizzle Sessions? You need to keep your "logs" together to promote the proper energy so your distributors will be more effective when talking to their friends.

It is not necessary to spend a lot of money for meeting facilities. There are many restaurants that have a back or side room you could use at no extra charge. Simply talk to the manager and explain to him you have a group of people you would like to get together with on a weekly basis. You start your meetings by 8:00 p.m. and you will be gone by 9:30. You will invite your people to come early (6:30 to 7:00) to have dinner before the meeting. He won't need to put on extra help since the orders can go in as they each arrive. Also, if the waitress gets busy, you are not concerned about speedy service. The restaurant manager and/or owner will be happy with this arrangement, and so will the waitress. Finally, be sure to encourage your people to tip well.

This arrangement should not cost you anything above your meals and tips. The distributors who do not wish to eat should come about 7:45.

We have found with this type of social setting it is very comfortable for your distributors to have a guest. You may even want to offer to buy your guest's dinner or coffee. (This makes your meals or coffees a deductible business expense.) Once they have signed up, they are on their own.

It is okay to invite your guest to your training meeting even if they have not yet seen your twenty-minute presentation. They will see it as the instructor is teaching the distributors how to present it. When making your invitations, emphasize that they are coming to a training session and not to an opportunity meeting. They will see the opportunity during the training.

# CHAPTER 15
## Important Phrases
## And Handling Objections

AS I POINTED OUT in Napkin Presentation #4, your business should look like a large building under construction. You can't see the building until it begins to rise, and it can't begin to rise until you have laid a solid foundation. In MLM you can't see your income (anything substantial) until you have laid your foundation there as well.

To a non-sales type, I say something like "I can see you have doubts about getting involved. I want you to understand that if you say 'yes' I will be training you. Also understand that if I didn't think you could do it, we would be talking about something else."

The question you should ask yourself about the above, is, **"Why would I want to talk someone into getting involved in my business if I didn't think they could do it?"** You may want to also mention, "Once you have been in the business thirty days and know just a fraction about the business that I do, you will understand why I am so excited about your opportunity.

**"Do I have to sell?"** No. The products will move in the process of building your business, sharing them with your friends. Have you ever seen a presentation of crystal, siding, cookware, fire alarms or vacuum cleaners? This is what most people think selling is. The definition of selling comes from 95% non-sales types and what they think selling is all about. They define selling as calling on strangers, trying to talk them into buying something they probably neither need nor want. You never have to do that in MLM. First, you are dealing with people you know: Second, you should be handling products they need and want.

**"Is it a pyramid?"** No. The major difference between MLM and pyramids is that pyramids are illegal. MLM has been around for over 50 years and if MLM were illegal, it would have been shut down long ago. When you get this objection, in most cases, I believe it is due to a fear of failure. The person you are dealing with is afraid to try your program and by asking if it is a pyramid, he thinks he will get you off his back because most distributors don't know how to respond.

**"I can't afford to go into business."** A person can get started in most MLM companies for under $100. Unless they want to spend the rest of their life working for someone else, they can't afford not to go into business. My definition of "having it made" is having more money than you can spend and the time to spend it. In my opinion it is a fact that you will never "have it made" working for somebody else.

**"My wife/husband won't be interested."** Don't let that hold you back. In most cases it is only one partner that initially gets a business started. Once it becomes successful, the other spouse will come on board. When this happens your business can really take off. In MLM when a couple builds their business together it's not 1 + 1= 2, it's 1 + 1= more. You get a synergistic effect that is really powerful.

**"Is there an advantage to being directly sponsored by a company?"** No. As a matter of fact, I would consider this to be a disadvantage. The more distributors you have between you and the company, the better. Everyone in your up-line should be helping and supporting your activities. When you are sponsored by the company, you are on your own.

**"How far down-group should I work?"** The further the better. Many distributors will not work beyond their pay-level. I think this is a mistake. Remember Napkin Presentation #9? When you work beyond your direct pay levels, you are putting heat under the distributors that you are getting paid on.

**"How do I select an MLM company?"** By the time you read this you will probably already be with a company. The truth is, most people don't pick their first company. Somebody they know who is already with a company, picked them.

**"Can I work with more than one program?"** To answer this properly, I need to divide companies into two categories. Major-effort programs, with break-aways and some minimum requirements, and the mail-order and uni-level types. Most people cannot handle more than one major-effort program. You could have several of the latter on your list as long as you understand that the activity with these programs should support your major effort program. There's an old saying that if you have lots of irons in the fire and one of them is hot, you don't need the rest. Most distributors who are in one major-effort program will gravitate toward spending their time with the one that works best for them.

**"I just don't have the time."** There are four elements to recruiting and sponsoring: 1) contacts, 2) time, 3) energy, and 4) knowledge. If I am dealing with a very busy person, I simply say, "I'm not asking for your time, just your contacts. Bring up the idea of MLM to your friends and have them contact me. In other words, we will use your contacts, my time, my energy, and my knowledge. You might spend two minutes, but I'll spend two hours."

**"What is the difference between recruiting and sponsoring?"** Recruiting is when you bring someone into your organization who is already experienced in Multi-Level Marketing (MLM). Sponsoring has the connotation of bringing someone new into MLM to whom you are making a commitment to train regarding how the industry operates. You can build quickly by recruiting. However, you can build solid by sponsoring.

**CONTEST IDEA:** Your people enter the contest by sponsoring someone who has never been in MLM. The new person signs a statement that this is their first company. You may enter as many times as you wish. As the new person reaches various achievement levels, the trainer would receive awards and prizes.

**"My sponsor doesn't help me. What should I do?"** Go up-line until you find someone who will. Eventually your sponsor, if inactive, will drop out, and you will move up-line under the one that is helping you.

**"How important are potlucks?"** Anytime you do something positive to bring your distributors together, you are creating energy.

**"There is a town about two hours drive from my home. I know five people there. Should I attempt to sponsor all five myself or should I sponsor one and put the rest under the one?"** You should never put anyone under anyone else unless you have brought the two parties together and there will be a mutual benefit and support. I would sponsor the best one first. Then, have some Sizzle Sessions so you can introduce the other four to the first one. If they get along, great. If they don't, you will end up doing the work anyway, so you may just as well sponsor them yourself.

**"My company says I can't join another company"** It is interesting to note that some companies have this attitude. They are happy to recruit distributors away from other companies, but it's a gross no-no if someone does it to them. These are the same companies that say, "Come with us and earn your freedom." As soon as you do, they are the ones who want to own you.

**"I am happy with my company, so why should I join another one?"** We believe in supporting our industry, MLM. When we want something for our family, we would prefer to join a company and buy the product wholesale; than buying from a retail or direct sales outlet. You can be signed up with a lot of companies to buy products wholesale, however, few distributors will be successful if they try to build an organization with more than one.

**"I am burned out on MLM. My company just declared Chapter 11."** This would be like going to town, eating out, getting a bad meal, then deciding that every restaurant in town is bad. Remember, you cannot fail in MLM. You can only quit. If your company goes belly-up, find another one. Never quit. On your tombstone visualize these two possible epitaphs: (Put your name in the blanks) A.) "Here Lies_____a person who tried once in life and quit," or B.) "Here lies _____a person who never made it, but never quit trying."

**"When should I quit my regular job?"** Many distributors get the urge to go full-time too soon. This is a major mistake. It puts too much pressure on them to make money NOW It is difficult to work on your foundation when the rent is due this week. You shouldn't quit your job until you have built up a reserve and you are making at least twice as much from your MLM efforts as you are from your regular job. Remember, your bonuses only come once a month (with most programs). Most people are used to getting paid weekly. Some spell it "weakly."

**"How would you graphically show the difference selling a lot and sponsoring a wide base 'A' vs. working with a few serious distributors (five at a time) down group 'B'."**

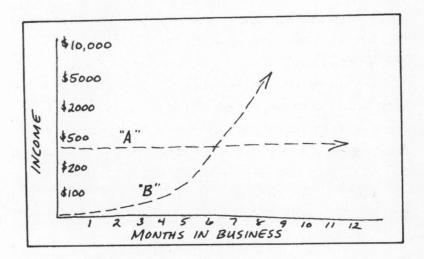

A distributor who sells a lot and sponsors a wide base would be on line "A". A distributor working the business with a few serious distributors would be on line "B". Ask your new distributor which line they would like to be on. When they say "B", you should ask them, "Do you understand that to be on line B you won't be making a lot of money for your first few months?" Again, you are trying to progam their mind for six months.

# NOTES

# CHAPTER 16
## Why Should 90% Of The Population Be In Network Marketing

Ninty percent of the population should be in Network marketing. When you understand the next presentation, you will see why.

In most Countries, the name of the game is to work until you retire and accumulate enough funds so you can live comfortably until you die. Living on social security would not be considered living comfortably. When you are living in the home of your choice (with no mortgage payment), driving the car of your choice (with no car payment); when your credit cards are all paid up and you have no phone bill–in other words, you have no bills - when you are in this situation and have $10,000 coming to you each and every month whether you get out of bed or not, you would have the lifestyle better than most millionaires.

For most people to have $10,000 coming in every month, it would take $2,400,000 in the bank at 5% interest. Refer to the Chart #1 (page 99) and you will see how much money it takes at various interest rates to produce various monthly incomes. Pick the income you would like to have, then see how much you would have to accumulate to be able to get it. Remember, before you can accumulate you have to make the money, pay your taxes, mortgage, car payment and all of your bills. How much do you really have left to accumulate?

So we now know it takes:
$2,400,000 to give you $10,000 per month.
Cut this in half-$1,200,000 to give you $5,000 per month.

How many people do you know who could accumulate $1,200,000 to $2,400,000 by the time they retire?

A person in network marketing can in 2 to 5 years build a part-time income of $5,000 to $10,000 per month. This money will spend the same as the money they would get from 5% interest on $1,200,000 to $2,400,000.

The above example is where you could be in 2 to 5 years with your residual income. Let's take a look at the first few months to one year: It takes $48,000 in the bank to produce a $200 monthly income. Assuming you are earning 5%. That is a STRETCH, because money earning in a typical bank is much less than that! How many people do you know that could save $48,000 in 3 months? Almost anyone, using our system, could build an organization that would pay them $200 per month.

Note the following:

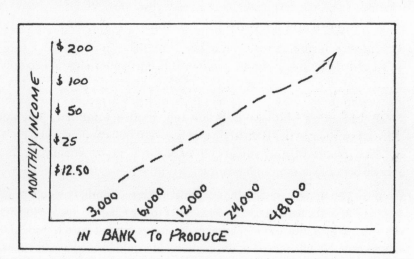

How many people do you know that could save $3,000 to $6,000 per month? Most people would say no one. How many people do you know that could sponsor one friend a month? Remember this only takes 45 seconds of talking, then loan them the book to read the first four napkin presentations. Then get them together with your sponsor. This can be done with a 3-way call. Isn't it interesting that anyone using this system can sponsor one friend a month and teach them to do the same.

Note: if you only sponsored one a month and taught your people to do the same, your organization would look like this:

| Month | Number of people in your Organization |
|-------|---------------------------------------|
| 1 | 2 |
| 2 | 4 |
| 3 | 8 |
| 4 | 16 |
| 5 | 32 |
| 6 | 64 |
| 7 | 128 |
| 8 | 256 |
| 9 | 512 |
| 10 | 1,024 |
| 11 | 2,048 |
| 12 | 4,096 |

What if you only did this once a year and taught your people to do the same? You would be financially independent by the end of 12 years. How many people would love to be retired in 12 years? One a month would get you there in 1 year!

Network Marketing is not a numbers game like sales. A salesperson goes to work for a sales manager. Network marketing is the opposite. When you sponsor someone, you get to go to work for them. You get to choose who you go to work for!

What you really need to do to be successful in network marketing can be said in two sentences:

1. Make a friend (if you don't have any).

2. Meet their friends.

# CHART #1- "Are You Secure In Your Retirement?"

Do you know how much money you need in the bank to receive the amount of interest you would like to have at retirement? To "own your own life" means you are able to do the things that you would like to do and not worry about the cost! The following chart shows the percentage of interest being paid by the financial institutions and the amount of money you need to invest to generate the monthly amount that meets your needs. Find the amount you would like to have, and then the current interest rate being paid by today's financial institutions, and see how much you need to save for retirement.

| $200 Per Month | | $600 Per Month | | $800 Per Month | | $1,000 Per Month | |
|---|---|---|---|---|---|---|---|
| Interest Rate | Amount in Bank | Interest Rate | Amount in Bank | Interest Rate | Amount in Bank | Interest Rate | Amount in Bank |
| 2% | $120,000 | 2% | $362,000 | 2% | $480,000 | 2% | $600,000 |
| 3 | 80,000 | 3 | 240,000 | 3 | 320,000 | 3 | 400,000 |
| 4 | 60,000 | 4 | 180,000 | 4 | 240,000 | 4 | 300,000 |
| 5 | 48,000 | 5 | 144,000 | 5 | 192,000 | 5 | 240,000 |
| 6 | 40,000 | 6 | 120,000 | 6 | 160,000 | 6 | 200,000 |
| 7 | 34,286 | 7 | 102,857 | 7 | 137,143 | 7 | 171,429 |
| 8 | 30,000 | 8 | 90,000 | 8 | 120,000 | 8 | 150,000 |
| 9 | 26,667 | 9 | 80,001 | 9 | 106,667 | 9 | 133,334 |
| 10 | 24,000 | 10 | 72,000 | 10 | 96,000 | 10 | 120,000 |

| $2,000 Per Month | | $4,000 Per Month | | $5,000 Per Month | | $10,000 Per Month | |
|---|---|---|---|---|---|---|---|
| Interest Rate | Amount in Bank | Interest Rate | Amount in Bank | Interest Rate | Amount in Bank | Interest Rate | Amount in Bank |
| 2% | $1,200,000 | 2% | $2,400,000 | 2% | $3,000,000 | 2% | $6,000,000 |
| 3 | 800,000 | 3 | 1,600,000 | 3 | 2,000,000 | 3 | 4,000,000 |
| 4 | 600,000 | 4 | 1,200,000 | 4 | 1,500,000 | 4 | 3,000,000 |
| 5 | 480,000 | 5 | 960,000 | 5 | 1,200,000 | 5 | 2,400,000 |
| 6 | 400,000 | 6 | 800,000 | 6 | 1,000,000 | 6 | 2,000,000 |
| 7 | 342,857 | 7 | 685,714 | 7 | 857,143 | 7 | 1,714,285 |
| 8 | 300,000 | 8 | 600,000 | 8 | 750,000 | 8 | 1,500,000 |
| 9 | 266,667 | 9 | 533,334 | 9 | 666,668 | 9 | 1,333,335 |
| 10 | 240,000 | 10 | 480,000 | 10 | 600,000 | 10 | 1,200,000 |

We have a system whereby you can go back to school a few hours per week to learn how to do it, get involved, and secure your financial security at whatever level you wish to work for. We know if you'll learn our system you could be financially independent in 1-3 years at better than $50,000.00 per year. How many college graduates go into debt for their education to get a good job, yet are not able to be financially independent in 1-3 years after graduation at $50,000.00 per year? I personally don't know any job, except a home-based business, that can give you this opportunity. If you would like to take advantage of OWNING YOUR OWN LIFE, contact the person who gave you this book.

# NOTES

# CHAPTER 17
## Vision for Lifestyle and Leadership

We've been traveling the world for 28 years. We are international lifestyle trainers and we teach people how to have a better quality of life through building successful network marketing organizations. We absolutely love what we do! And that is because when you are successful in network marketing, you are well and happy. The fact of the matter is, in network marketing you don't work hard for a living, you build smart for a lifestyle. Now is the time to start a better life for yourself and your family. Now is the time to get the stress out of your life. Now is the time to do something different. If you don't know what you want, and you don't know where you are going, then you will be lost. And you for sure will not be living your dreams. Now is the time to change, and network marketing can help you make those changes.

Nancy's life is just one example. She spent seven years grinding her way up in the corporate world, hitting her head on the glass ceiling. She and I both know what it's like not to own your life. And let me tell you, once she got into network marketing everything changed for the better—that's why it is so important for people to understand this business. Let me give you another example of a woman I met in Thailand. She was working in a factory and she was making the equivalent of about $120 a month. After this woman got the vision of network marketing and learned what she needed to do, she was making over $20,000 every month. Another example is a woman I met in New York. She worked in a bank and made over $100,000 a year, but she had no time. She really wanted to have a relationship, she wanted to have some children, but she didn't have time for any of this. She had money, but no time. She attended one of our networking trainings and she got the vision of what she wanted to do. She knew she could make more money in networking so she started building her business in network marketing. Today she is married, has a family, and makes more money. She owns her life.

Whatever you want out of life, whatever you want to contribute to life, you have that opportunity in network marketing. And to be successful, the first thing you must do is to have a dream that is really important to you. In other words, what do you want? What do you really want most out of life? You may want good health and more energy, or maybe you'd like a residual income so that you don't have to worry about paying bills. Maybe you want peace of mind, or a loving relationship. What about a vacation or a sports car or a new home? Maybe you have a special cause or a charity that needs time or funding. Maybe you want to spend more time at your church or focus more on saving the environment. You may want more money and more time for any number of reasons. Whatever they are, if you want these things, you have the opportunity to make them happen. Prosperity can come into your life. You have a choice today. You've got to get the vision. Once you know you have a choice, nothing will hold you back. I suggest you take a picture of what you want—an actual photograph. Keep it where you can see it. This will help to make it real and keep it in the forefront of your mind. I must say, every picture that I have ever put on our refrigerator has come true. Dreams can become realities, sooner than you might think. It's like magic. Your vision leads you to success. It's absolutely amazing what can happen. And always remember, after you reach one dream, move on to the next dream. Your dreams will just keep coming true, if you keep choosing the life you desire.

## Why Network Marketing?

I think everyone should be in network marketing. That's my dream and my goal, to get everyone that has any entrepreneurial spirit at all into network marketing. All they have to do is understand it and believe it. And if they understand it, they are going to believe it! So many people are already involved in network marketing and building huge businesses. I know lots of them! In network marketing, you don't have a boss; you are your own boss; you are self-employed. That is why you need self-discipline. You must be self-motivated. After traveling the world for all these many years, I have discovered that people want two important things from building a home-based networking business: 1) they want some money in their pocket as soon as possible, so that they can have a better life; and 2) they want a fun opportunity. Too many people have miserable jobs, and too many others don't even have a job at all. The thing to realize is that with network marketing you can make a good living and have fun doing it. You can start part-time and build from there.

There are six major areas in your life. They are:
1) God
2) Family
3) Work
4) Social
5) Financial
6) Physical

All these areas work together to make you well and happy. And you can be a leader in each area of your life. You can actually achieve balance in your life. With network marketing, you can live the life you dream about, and have a lot of fun doing it! When you are a leader, you learn how to think smart, build smart and be smart. You can truly make a difference in your own life and the lives of others. So it's time to reinvent and reconstruct your life. It's time to pick yourself up, dust yourself off and make a new life for yourself, your family and your friends. You can do it, because the tools are there to help you. Now is the time to lead yourself and show your team that you can lead them to the next level in your company. If you don't have a team, now is the time to start building one. Networking is a very social and fun opportunity. You're going to love it! It is a business model that can change your life and that of everyone you know. People are already doing it. Now is the time for you to go do it. People are losing their jobs, people are living in fear. You don't have to live like that. You have a choice today. It's time to create an opportunity.

Remember, your attitude and your actions speak louder than your words. Your attitude comes across first and your success will follow. And what kind of attitude do you need? You need a positive attitude in every aspect, and you need to have passion about your dreams and what it takes to make them real. Along with that, you need to develop the traits of a good leader. In network marketing you do not work alone—you create a team that works with you, and you lead them along with you on the road to success.

## 7 Steps to Becoming a Good Leader

### 1. BECOME ACTIVELY INVOLVED

You sponsor a friend in your company, and you help that friend sponsor their friend, and it just keeps going. You teach and nurture your team to be a success; you share a proven system that will make them successful. This way they can duplicate their efforts and grow very fast and strong. You are the role model, and your team will follow. In a networking family, you teach and nurture each person along the road to success. Of course, you have to take one step at a time, and sometimes its baby steps. Sometimes you might even fall down. But you get back up and you learn from your mistakes, and you keep going. You are a leader; you never give up! Soon your team will start multiplying and your organization will be growing faster and faster, and stronger and stronger. You will really start to have fun, helping others and making money yourself.

I like to compare network marketing to making popcorn. Whether you cook the popcorn in a pan, or in a bag in the microwave, you've got to get some heat under it first. In network marketing, the heat comes when people have the vision and passion for what they're doing. Once it starts getting hot in the pan or in the bag, the popcorn starts popping. It just pops a little bit to begin with, and then it starts popping like crazy. It's just popping and popping and the bag fills up and popcorn is just overflowing out of the pan. Network marketing is the same. It starts off slow in the beginning. You're not making a whole lot of money and maybe not helping a whole lot of people. But then, all of a sudden, it takes off. And boy does it take off! Your life will be overflowing. Just keep at it. Too many times have I seen people quit right before things get moving. That is why it is important to understand the network marketing business, and it is crucial that you have the tools you need to succeed.

## 2. HAVE A "LEADER'S ATTITUDE"

You must have the vision and focus to want to be a leader. In network marketing, helping people be successful is your number one concern and responsibility. You need to work on yourself and grow and develop into a highly effective and caring individual. Networking is a relationship business; we change people's lives one person at a time. What is so great is that what you learn in building your networking business, you can use in all aspects of your life.

## 3. GET ORGANIZED

When you are organized, you cannot only lead yourself, but you can lead others, too. Clean up your car, your closet, your office, your drawers, your desk, your garage, your purse, your wallet, your kids, your home, and your yard. When you are organized, you feel good about yourself and your surroundings. When you feel good, you can help others feel good and have a better life. Remember as a leader, you are a role model. You lead by example. You can't teach somebody something that you don't know or can't do yourself. You have to know what you are doing.

## 4. BE FLEXIBLE

Things are always changing, aren't they? It is fun and good to learn new things, and if you have a positive attitude it's very easy to be flexible. A leader is always adapting and addressing life's changes. You have to constantly adjust to different situations, circumstances and conditions. Of course, you always stay focused on the goal, and remain consistent with your purpose and your vision of the future. There are many ways to meet your goals, if you are flexible. Remember life is a journey, not a destination

## 5. COMMUNICATE, COMMUNICATE, COMMUNICATE

The best communicators are also the best listeners. I have found that lack of communication is a huge problem, in all areas of life. As a leader, it is very important to keep in touch with your family of team members. As the leader, you keep them on track and inspire them to keep moving forward, one step at a time. As a leader, you help them to know what they want. A lot of people don't have any idea what their purpose is; they are just drifting. That's where communication comes in. Start asking questions. Start teaching. Start sharing.

## 6. MANAGE YOUR TIME EFFECTIVELY

Time waits for no one. The following list contains some of the skills you should develop to help you best utilize your time:
• Prioritize
• Multi-task
• Always be on time or early
• Delegate

As your networking family starts to grow, your time will become more and more valuable. Time is your most important and precious resource; use it well, and let every minute count.

## 7. INSPIRE OTHERS TO ACTION

If a person really wants something they don't already have, they just need a plan. Help your distributor write a mission statement. This statement is his or her purpose and goal in life. We have a mission statement that is to help as many people as we can, and to have a better quality of life through network marketing.

## It's Your Opportunity: Take Advantage of It!

Getting involved in network marketing can be the most exciting and fun way of life in the world. It is our world and it can be your world too. The door is wide open. Wherever we travel we have a team, a family, to visit. How great it is to have friends everywhere we go! And the best part is you can have it, too. To be a leader in networking, all you need to do is train your family of distributors to be successful, and that is so easy! It is simple and fun and anyone can do it. The reason it is so easy is because there are tools that do all the training and teaching for you. All you have to know is the system that we share with you in this book. Take yourself through the system, and then teach others to do the same. Everything is there for you. You can be a leader in all aspects of your life if you care enough about other people. Your integrity will show through, and they will follow you, because in network marketing you can live the life you dream about. Now is the time.

# NOTES

# NOTES

# CHAPTER 18
## Let the Tools Do the Talking

This is a special chapter put together based on the training offered by Don Failla on getting the tools to work for you. We have included it in this special edition because we feel that it will give you that little extra help. "Kick-start" your business today.

Travelling for more than 30 years has shown us how a duplicatable system truly makes a difference in people's lives.

If you consider that a brand new person can take in enough information in 10 minutes or less to actually start sponsoring and building a business, the system becomes invaluable. The system is so simple that anybody in the world can build a network marketing business, if they want to.

This is covered in my book called The System, but we decided to put this chapter in this book to give you that "kick-start" we mentioned.

We have learned that only 5% of any population are sales types. Therefore 95% are part of the non-sales types. The non-sales types think that sales is talking somebody into something that they don't really need or want.

Furthermore, Nancy and I got rich through network marketing by working with the non-sales types. There are two reasons for this:

1. There are more of them to talk to.
2. There is no competition.

Unfortunately 90% of the people in network marketing think they're looking for sales types. Sales types are normally fickle and opportunistic. As soon as someone else comes along with a fair deal, you have lost them. It is important to realize that people in network marketing are looking for sales types because they don't understand the business. Historically sales types have the least chance of making it in this business. It is ironic that people spend most of their time looking for the type of person to join their business who has the least chance of making it.

On the other hand, if you happen to be a sales type, you are in the right place. A sales type person can make it really big in network marketing on one single condition. That condition is that they are prepared to learn how network marketing really works. Most sales people do not know or understand network marketing.

This is a business about duplication

Sales people have been "recruited" throughout their life. They are "recruited" by sales managers to sell for them. If you "recruit" a sales person into your business he thinks he can go out and find people to sell for him. With that mindset he will never make it in this business because we do not "recruit" people—we "sponsor" them. Note the difference—sponsoring means we go to work for them! The idea is that you sponsor someone, you meet their friends, you teach them how to sponsor someone and then they go to work for those they have sponsored, just like you worked for them during the sponsoring process.

The biggest asset sales people have over non-sales types is the ability to call on and meet strangers. It's that same asset that becomes the cause of their failure in this business. It is so easy for them to meet people that they just run around signing people up ... they don't spend enough quality time with any one person so that they can help that person actually get started in building a business, i.e. SPONSOR them.

We have seen sales people come into this business and recruit 100 people. After 6 months they are but 1 or 2 levels deep in just a couple of places. They haven't duplicated themselves at all and give up or move on to the next opportunity.

The way to establish whether you are duplicated in this business is when the person you sponsored is 3 levels deep. If you hold up your hand and assume that you are the thumb, the first finger represents the person you sponsor. When you can put a name to each of the other 3 fingers down the line you are 3 levels deep. Only once you have achieved this can you consider yourself duplicated in the first person you sponsored. If you look at it diagrammatically, you will actually be 4 levels deep.

It is uncomfortable for non-sales types to call on and meet strangers. So what they do is sponsor a friend and then they help them with their friends and they help them with their friends. This process is much slower but it gains momentum because the game of multiplication is played successfully. The sales people are always playing the game we call dividing and subtracting. We want to multiply in this business. In fact you can break the business down into two simple sentences: You make a friend and meet their friends. You make a friend and meet their friends.

As mentioned, for non-sales types it is very uncomfortable to call on leads and if you do the business the way that we teach it, you will never have to worry about leads again. When you sponsor someone, that person will know a couple of people you don't know and all you need to do is teach them what you already have. Learn how to talk to the people you already know, using the tools to do most of the talking and when the timing is right they can introduce them to you.

In all our network marketing years, we've been involved with health products; however, we never think of ourselves as selling health products. The reason for this is, no matter how fantastic your products may be, if you think you're selling health products you are in for a difficult time. Only 15% of the population are either sick, hurt or into health. Only 8% of these are really into health. Therefore, if you think you're selling health products then you're looking for that 8%. Considering the amount of network marketing companies and health food stores out there, you have to be really knowledgeable on what you are offering to be able to get the kind of sales that is desired. We don't have to do that. We don't have to take the time to learn about all the products because in reality we are not selling health products.

Now you may ask the question, "What are we doing and what should I be doing?"

If you want to build the business fast, you are looking for people who want "something." We call it "Own Your Life." We have a pin … it says "Own Your Life," (available at www.45SecondTools.com) which means having the money and time to do what you want to do. If 15% of the people are either sick, hurt or are into health, 95% of any population of people want a better life. "They want something." The other 5% already have it. They already have the time, they already have the money and they'd like to live forever and they'll buy anything you have.

A few years ago we were in Copenhagen, Denmark driving up the coast to Helsingborg and had to take the ferry across to Sweden. It's a 20 minute crossing and it was a Friday. Driving up the coast we could literally see tens of thousands of yachts. When we got onto the ferry, we looked out over the water and we could not see a single yacht on the water. We couldn't see any because they were all in the marines, and they were all in the marines because all the people were at their jobs.

Question: Why would I go down to the marines to talk to people about health products knowing that only 15% are sick, hurt or into health? What these people really want is to get their yacht out onto the water Monday through Friday! We go to the marines to talk to people about what they want and then we show them how to get it by using the System.

In the same line of thinking … people like to ski. Would you like to ski on the weekends or Monday to Friday when it's not crowded? Without a doubt, Monday to Friday is the best time!

Our philosophy is very simple. We look for someone who wants something. Whether they can sell or not makes no difference. In fact, as I've already mentioned, if they are in sales we've got a little extra training to do.

I don't mind making the following statement because I feel it is absolutely true. "100% of the people in the world that are not in network marketing do not understand it!" 80% – 90% of the people in network marketing don't even understand it. What we want to do is have people read my book. When they read the book, they will understand network marketing and when they understand it, they will get involved. Once they've read my book we call them people who "know how to drive."

## The System

The system involves 3 simple steps. If you ask people who have been in network marketing for a while how much training time it takes before their new person can go out and sponsor someone, they will tell you, "It doesn't take 1 or 2 hours, or 1 or 2 days. It literally takes weeks and months!" Very often their new recruits never sponsor anyone and drop out of the business. The reason that they haven't sponsored somebody is very simple. They haven't sponsored anyone because nobody has taught them something that THEY CAN DO!

Everybody thinks that their vehicle is the hottest vehicle on the planet. Now when I talk about vehicle, I'm referring to your company, your products and your marketing plan.

In a network marketing presentation, half an hour to two hours is spent on telling people all about the vehicle, the company, products and marketing plan. People get all excited and when they sign up they think that particular vehicle is like a Lamborghini. You will agree that a Lamborghini is a hot vehicle! When they go out the next day and start speaking, to what could be their hottest prospects, they get shot down and they get burnt, over and over. They are crashing and burning all over the place for one simple reason: THEY DON'T KNOW HOW TO DRIVE.

As mentioned, when you understand network marketing we say you "know how to drive." So if you owned a Lamborghini, a brand new one, would you allow your best friend to go for a drive around the block in your brand new Lamborghini if he didn't know how to drive? Obviously you wouldn't do that. It's the same with network marketing. We never show anyone our vehicle until they know how to drive!

A lot of people will tend to allude or know what the product is. Let me re-assure you, the very second you mention one product from your company, they think that you're trying to sell them something or that you are trying to get them to sell for you. At this point you've lost them. We don't want you to experience that. That's why we wear the "Own Your Life" pin so that we can get people talking about the right thing, about lifestyle and people wanting things. This way we get people off on the right foot.

Here's another analogy that goes along with this. Trying to sell a product in network marketing is like lifting up the hood of the car, taking the whole engine apart and putting it back together again before you can even start talking about the business. With the System, it's like handing you the keys to the vehicle and letting you start the car and drive down the highway as you get started with your business immediately. While you're doing that, you're learning everything you need to know about the company, products and marketing plan from your CD player.

Can you see the difference? With the first approach you have to get to know everything about the products, company and marketing plan before you can do anything. With the System you don't have to know anything and you can start building your business.

Keep in mind that there are 2 reasons why people start dropping out with any company.

1. They're not making money.
2. They haven't had an experience with the product.

If you can show people a way they can sponsor someone in their first or second day in the business which will bring them a little bit of income credited for their effort, whether it be $5 or $20 or $50, it doesn't matter how much, they're going to get excited. The mere fact that they're going to get a check will get them to stick around a little longer which will allow them time to experience the product.

This is the basic philosophy. All you need to do is show people "how to drive" before you show them the vehicle.

Finally, here's how the System works.

## PERSON-TO-PERSON APPROACH

This is strictly a warm market approach. Once you know how the System works we will cover briefly how to work it with your cold market at the end of this chapter.

Let's say you are talking to people who are friends—people you already know. For example, I've known my friend Tom for many years. We are in the restaurant for coffee, breakfast, or dinner. IMPORTANT: You start this process when you're leaving the restaurant. If you start as soon as you sit down you're exposing yourself to needing to answer a lot of questions that you might not be able to answer.

On your way out, you say to Tom, "Hey Tom, you might be able to help me out. Do you know anyone that likes to travel and go on vacation?"

I have never ever got NO as an answer to that question. Note that I didn't ask Tom whether HE would like to go on vacation. I asked whether he knows someone that would. He would say something like: "Yeah I do, or everybody does," etc.

Then I say, "Tom, it takes 3 things to do that. It takes time, it takes money, and it takes your health. If I can show YOU how you could have all 3, would you be interested?"

Notice that I flip over from asking if he knew anybody to the first person. "If I could show YOU." Again, people won't say NO to that. At this point I would hand him my lifestyle card business card (available at www.45SecondTools.com) and on the back of the card is the 45 Second Presentation.

## TELEPHONE APPROACH

Let's say I'm talking to Tom on the phone. It doesn't matter if he's in Europe or on the next block. You can use the System with anyone, anywhere.

When you're about ready to hang up the phone you simply say, "Tom, have you ever thought what it would be like if you could own your life?"

After I say that there is usually a long silence.

Break the silence and say:

"Tom, what I think it means to own your life is by the time you subtract out all the sleeping time, commuting time, working time and things that you have to do each and every day of your life, most people don't have one or two hours a day of their lives to do what they would like to do. And then would they have the money to do it?

"We have discovered a way a person can learn how to own their life by building a home-based business and we have a system for doing it that is so simple, anyone can do it, it doesn't require any selling and the best part is it won't take much of your time.

"If you're interested I'll get you some information."

You will recognize this as "the 45 Second Presentation." It's called that because it takes 45 seconds to say. The number one excuse people have for not doing this business is, "I don't have time."

Last summer, we were in Kazan, Russia, about 600 miles outside Moscow. We spoke to 6000 distributors. I asked them, "How many of you have had people tell you they don't have time to do this business?" Every single person raised their hands. They raised both hands! It's the biggest excuse people have for not doing the business. With our system we never get that excuse because we don't take their time. It takes 30 seconds to read the card. "If you're interested I'll get you some information."

After hearing me say "the 45 Second Presentation," Tom is interested. At this point I loan Tom a copy of The 45 Second Presentation That Will Change Your Life book and get him to read the first 4 chapters. Never tell someone to read the whole book. It goes on the shelf and they get to it "in due time." Tell them to read the first 4 chapters and they'll look at it and see the diagrams and they will quickly realize that they can read it in a short time. IF they want something they will finish the book in one sitting. You know 3 things if they finish the book: (1) They want something; (2) You have someone who now understands network marketing; and (3) They now know how to drive!

This is the very reason why our approach is called the Own Your Life Plan. Our book has sold over 5.5 million copies. 70% of the people who read the book the first time never paid for it. Someone loaned them the book. When they read the book they realize how great it is because they don't have to spend time in the future explaining the business. It used to take us 3 to 4 hours and many more of extended training to teach the business to people. We did it for 10 years and got burned out. By then we got smart and made a tape. From the tape, the book was written and now we simply loan them the book.

Therefore, you have 1 of 2 choices. You can learn everything in the book and you can meet with someone and spend 3 to 4 hours with them, teaching them what is written in the book, or you can loan them the book.

A few notes about the 3 steps:

**Step 1:** Use your lifestyle business card. Hand them the card so that they can read the 45 Second Presentation printed on the back. If you're speaking to them on the phone, you can read it to them.

**Step 2:** Hand them the book/e-book. If you're on the phone, you can mail them the book, and if you mail the book, I would recommend that you use Priority Mail because this puts a little urgency on the matter. Most people aren't used to getting Priority Mail.

We are ready for step 3.

**Step 3:** Your vehicle. Your company, product and marketing plan. I tell people this: "Show me a business in your town that started for $100 or $150 (whatever your business starts with) with a monthly overhead of $100, $200 or $300." Everybody knows what overheads are in a business. I say: "You know, that is all it costs to get started with our business and with the monthly overhead you're going to get some great products that are going to make you feel better and you're going to absolutely love them. Here's my website." Give them your website from your company and have them check it out. Once they've checked it out they can get back to you with questions.

IMPORTANT: When you give them your website, tell them you'll take care of their questions. Don't tell them that you will answer them because you might have just started in your business and won't be able to answer them. Say you'll take care of them. That means that if you don't have the answers to their questions you'll get your sponsor on the phone or their sponsor on the phone, so that they can help you answer those questions.

That's it!

## WHAT DOESN'T WORK.

Here's an example: We are on a flight to Florida. We fly United and we have plenty of miles so we upgrade to first class. We have seats 1A and 1B. Nancy is in 1B. She gets up and goes to the restroom and stands in the alley to stretch her legs. The flight attendant and sky marshal are sitting in the jump seat having their meal. The flight attendant looks up and says to Nancy "Can I get you something?" Nancy says, "No, that's fine, I'm just stretching my legs but I should ask you … can I get you something?" She says "Yes …lots of money!" (This seems to be the first thing on people's minds when you ask that question—and it makes them laugh which initiates a pleasant conversation.)

Nancy says, "Well I can do that!" So she went to her seat and got her card, her lifestyle card, handed it to her and said, "When you have a minute, read the back of the card and when you get home check out my website" We use the IOwnMyLife.net prospecting website rather than our company site. This kind of website is very useful with your cold market.

The internet is a wonderful system; HOWEVER, it doesn't work if you think you can send out 50,000 emails to people you don't know. They wouldn't sign up in droves for your opportunity and live happily ever after. The reason it doesn't work is because nobody has made a connection. Anybody that signs up with someone off the internet this way normally doesn't end up buying anything and they don't stay around very long.

We encourage you to take hold of the System and build a powerful business in this wonderful industry. We hope to meet you on one of our next "unconventions."

# NOTES

# NOTES

# APPENDIX 1
## How To Use The Own Your Life Pin
## And Other 45 Second Tools

Nancy and I wear the Own Your Life pin everywhere we go. When people ask us about the pin we tell them that "Owning Your Life" is having the time and money to do what you want to do,, when you want to do it. This also allows us to start a conversation and ask the person a question–"Do you know anyone that likes to travel and go on holiday?" Now I am right into the steps of the system. The pin gives us an opportunity to get started talking to our prospect about lifestyle first. If we wore a pin that has our company name on it and they ask what it is then we end up starting with step three first: talking about our company and products. As soon as you mention a product to them they think you are trying to sell them something.

You should get everyone in your organization wearing the pin. This will benefit your whole organization. Let me give you an example. Nancy and I go on a lot of cruises. If we are by ourselves on a cruise and there are 3,000 other passengers we might get a few people during the course of the week that will ask us about the pin. But when we are having an "unconvention" cruise and we have thirty or forty people with us and they are all wearing the pin then everyone gets 50 to 60 people asking about it. With 40 people wearing the pin and moving around the other 3,000 passengers see the pin everywhere. Their curiosity about the pin goes up so high that they want to know what it means.

What I just described about wearing the pin on a cruise will also work in your own area. If you are the only one wearing it you will get people from time to time asking you about it. If you get everyone in your group wearing it all the time, this will increase the curiosity in your community and your whole organization will benefit.

People ask us what the pin is made of and we say solid gold. Then we tell them that we are just kidding but the pin is worth more then solid gold. If one person asks you about it and you get into the right conversation with them and they come into your business then that can be worth way more than solid gold.

People all over the world wear the pin. It is very popular in Japan and Germany even though the pin is in English. When someone in Japan is wearing a pin in English it just raises the curiosity. In Denmark they wear the pin upside down. Nancy said to them, "Why are you wearing the pin upside down?" The answer was that when people see it they want to straighten it and then they ask about it. It is a perfect segue way into the System.

When Nancy is shopping or in the grocery store and she notices someone looking at the pin but they are too shy to ask about it, she simply says to them, "I bet you want to know what that means." She can then hand them her card with The 45 Second Presentation on it. It is a great way to make new contacts and friends. Remember the first thing you have to do with someone you meet is to make a connection with them. You need to make a friend. The pin is a great door opener.

With the right tools this business can be a lot of fun and can grow very fast.

Refer to Chapter VII (page 43) for review of getting into a general discussion about MLM and setting up a time to get together to explain the whole story about the program you're involved in.

DON'T try to explain the entire marketing plan on a street corner or when your prospect is supposed to be working,

Distributors ask, "At what point do I show the new person the Napkin Presentations?" The answer is simple, "I don't." I give them a book and a CD and I set a time in the near future when I can get back with them and discuss the material. Once they have listened to the CD and read the book, there isn't that much to discuss. Now it's time to sponsor them and get to work helping them to sponsor someone else.

By giving your prospect The 45 Second Presentation book and CD, that gets them through the material twice. The second time through they will get more out of it. If you just give them the book, it's unlikely that they will read it twice, or in the case of giving them the CD only, that they would listen to it twice. Also consider the fact that you don't know whether the person gets more form listening or reading. If they do both, it's almost guaranteed they will take in enough information to convince them that Multi-Level marketing is something that even they can do successfully.

I suggest that you purchase ten sets of The 45 Second Presentation book and the CDs to supply your down-line. The sooner you put these tools to work for you, the sooner you put these tools to work for you, the sooner your organization will grow. Again, TEACH your people the steps to success. These books and CDs will teach them the fundamentals. Then, you can follow up by sharing your personal success experiences.

You can have the most fantastic "vehicle" in the industry, but until your distributors or representatives know how to "drive." They are simply not going to get anywhere.

When you teach distributors or representatives the presentations in this book, you are teaching them truly how to "drive." Bringing a new person on your "vehicle" without teaching them to "drive" is a waste of time–yours and theirs!

The 45 Second Presentation that Will Change Your Life should be used as a give-away for your new distributors. When they are ready to learn more, they can purchase the 45 Second Toolbox that contains all of the Failla training tools.

*-Don Failla*

# APPENDIX 2
## How To Build A Successful MLM Business . . . The Fun, Fast Way!

## Here Are 5 Easy Steps

1. Talk to a friend about owning their own life. Give them your lifestyle card and send them to your IOwnMyLife.net website. This step takes only 5 minutes.

2. Help them to understand MLM. Loan your friend Don Failla's *The 45 Secound Presentation That Will Change Your Life* book with companion CD. This step takes 1 minute.

3. Look for commitment. Ask your friend, 'Would you be willing to go back to school for 5 to 10 hours a week for 6 months to learn how to own your own life?" (30 seconds!)
If they answer Yes- Go to step 4
If they answer NO- Share your products or service and get a friend-customer, and a referral. This step takes 2 minutes.

4. Share your vehicle (company, products, marketing plan). Initial presentation on vehicle should take only 15 minutes maximum. Sign up new distributor.

5. Have your new distributor repeat the above steps with their friends.

## How To Work Smart

There are 3 elements to building a successful organization:

1. The Vehicle (company, products, marketing plan)

2. The Gas (motivational books, CDs, speakers, sponsor, contests, rallies, etc.)

3. How to Drive (understanding MLM)
   • Let the MLM Training Tools do the work for you, and save you time,
   • If your prospect starts asking a lot of questions, tell them that's what the 5 to 10 hours per week are all about. Your prospect does not need to know everything to get started.

## Don And Nancy Failla's Philosophy

Take 15 minutes to find out if a person would be willing to take the time to learn how to drive the vehicle before you waste 1 to 4 hours telling them about it.

# APPENDIX 3
## The Gallery of Gems: Key Ideas And Fun Phrases By Don & Nancy Failla

The following are some of our favorite phrases (a few are just fun, most have a nugget of wisdom), as well as some of the core ideas we've incorporated into our successful business. And here's a suggestion. Gather some friends around in a Sizzle Session, and read and discuss these statements. It can stimulate a lot of fun thoughts and ideas of your own.

## Don's Favorites

- If you want your dreams to come true, then wake up.
- Make a friend, meet their friends.
- Teach your people how to do this, and then do that.
- Anyone who thinks Networking has anything to do with sales will never make it big in this business, with very few exceptions.
- The computer is a great asset to building your business so at least learn to do emails.
- Non-sales types think selling is talking someone into something they do not need or want.
- This is a sponsor and teach business, not a recruit and sell business.
- Network Marketing is building a family of consumers.
- You don't recruit people to sell for you, sponsor people so you can go to work for them.
- You are not duplicating unless the person you sponsor is 3 levels deep.
- The secret to The System is not to talk; let the tools do the talking.

- The more you talk, the more your prospect thinks they don't have time, then they think they cannot do what you're doing.
- Salesmen can be huge in this business, provided they are willing to learn this business.
- The number-one excuse people have for not doing the business is time.
- Anyone can meet a stranger if someone will introduce the stranger to them.
- Watch out for eavesdroppers.
- If you can't talk to your friends about your Networking business, then you either don't believe it or don't understand it.
- When one understands this business, we then say they know how to drive.
- If you want to see a pyramid, go to Egypt.
- To duplicate down more than two levels you need a simple System.
- You can teach your friend The System in less than ten minutes.
- Eliminate the word sell from your vocabulary.
- Five percent of any population are the good sales types; 95 percent are the non-sales types. Learn to build with the non-sales types there's no competition and there are more of them to talk to.
- Teach your prospects how to drive before you show them your vehicle.
- Would you let your best friend go for a drive around the block in your brand new hot sports car if they did not know how to drive?
- You can work hard in the beginning for almost nothing and hardly work at all in the future and make a fortune.
- Making one new friend can make a difference.
- The more you know, the slower you grow.
- Only take advice from people who are currently building a business.
- A hundred-name list is sales talk, not Network Marketing.
- A short list is okay.
- Teach the people you already have how to talk to people they already know.
- If you're doing the business right, you never have to look for strangers.

- Your acre of diamonds is the people you already know.
- A sizzle session is about getting together to share ideas.
- When you have a job you are helping someone else reach their dreams.
- Find someone who wants something then show them how The System can help them get it.
- Two things happen when you talk too much to your prospect. They think they don't have time and they think they cannot do what you're doing.
- The Own Your Life movement is on around the world.
- The Own Your Life pin is not made from solid gold however it is worth much more.
- Without a map you could get lost.
- Real men don't ask directions.
- It is hard to teach salespeople not to talk.
- This business is about multiplication not addition and subtraction.
- What do you want?
- Sell your products or service to a non-sales type first, and they will always think this is a selling business.
- Network Marketing and sales mix like oil and water they don't.
- There are Network Marketing companies, and there are direct sales companies and they're different.
- Let the tools do the work for you.
- Your best tool is your sponsor.

## Nancy's Favorites

- Don't work hard for a living, work smart for a lifestyle.
- Money isn't everything, but it sure keeps you in touch with the kids and grand kids.
- What you do today will determine your future.
- The time for women is now.

- Why isn't everyone in Network Marketing?
- Better in the morning to be able to roll over than to roll out when the alarm goes off.
- You can be there to see your children grow up.
- It's all about fun, happiness and a healthy lifestyle.
- Times are always changing and it's good to learn new things.
- Your dreams can come true if you get the vision of Network Marketing.
- You never know when you are going to meet your next best friend or get your next best idea.
- You either want to own your life or you don't, it's your choice.
- Network Marketing is a paid social life.
- Do something fun every day.
- Lifestyle is something everyone wants to have and you can have it!
- I have never met a man who doesn't like working with a woman, especially if she is making him money.
- Your journey in life is about the choices you have made.
- Life is like a book, if you don't travel you only read one page.
- Take back your vacation/holiday.
- A good attitude can make a huge difference.
- You can make it in Network Marketing if you use the tools and never give up.
- What would your life look like if time and money were not a problem?
- Network Marketing is the greatest gift you can give a friend.
- You can create a second income without a second job.
- Time is our most precious and limited resource.
- If you really want something, you can make it in Network Marketing.
- Some people travel in their mind, some people travel in their heart, and some people actually go somewhere.
- Women are the best because they have the nature to nurture.
- You are never too old to get started.

- Experience is your best teacher.
- There is no substitute for experience.
- What is the joy in your life?
- Think smart, build smart, be smart.
- Choose to be happy and positive.
- Fun to be free.
- Welcome to freedom.
- Why keep working for a living when you can work for a lifestyle and really make a difference.
- Stress is the number-one killer.
- We're in the people business; we change peoples lives one person at a time.
- Keep it simple, make it fun and people will want to join you.
- Don't take yourself so seriously. Lighten up and have fun.
- The more fun you have, the more successful you will be.
- In Networking, you have more fun per hour.
- Having fun is your full time business.
- There are a lot of lonely people that should join a Networking company.
- Be a good listener.
- There is a light at the end of the tunnel.
- Learn to ask questions.
- You are not going to get out of this world alive so you might as well go for it.
- One life, live it.
- One life, own it.
- Almost everyone would like to travel.
- Cruising is good for the soul.
- Shopping is a good thing.
- Living on a budget is malo (Spanish for bad).

## Don & Nancy's Favorites

- Are you sick and tired of being sick and tired?
- We are not on vacation, this is how we live.
- Breaking the home barrier is being at home wherever you are.
- We ate at sixty-five Chart House restaurants in eighteen months and received two sets of tickets to fly around the world free.
- We are lifestyle trainers and we teach people how to have a better life.
- Without time, money and your health, you really don't have much of a life.
- The audio version of the 45 Second Presentation book is for people who can't read, don't like to read, don't have time to read, or are blind.
- The power of one is huge.
- Children can be great motivators.
- International travel only take what you can carry yourself.
- Mistakes can cost you time and money.
- Timing is very important.
- Listening is more important than talking.
- We like to teach our people that anyone can do The System.
- Traveling with a purpose is better than traveling as a tourist.
- Wear the Own Your Life pin every day.
- We travel so much our whole life is a write-off.
- We chose Richard Rabbit as our mascot because rabbits multiply so fast.
- Having The System will make you confident.

I was introduced to The 45 Second Presentation that Will Change Your Life by my sister and business partner. She happened on an old copy in a used book store. Little did either of us realize how that book would change the shape of our businesses. It didn't take long to see that what Mr. Failla talks about in the book was the piece of our business that had been missing. We've been so impressed with his information that we asked him to speak at a seminar. I believe that his book is a tool that everyone should have in their toolbox!

**– Brenda Jumpa**

Don Failla's book has done just what the title suggests—it has changed our lives and the lives of many in our organization. Without a doubt, it has been the main reason our organization has excelled so rapidly in our particular industry.

We continually use the system in this book to teach and train those who we sponsor in our business. We give the book to each new person who signs on with us. It is our "manual" for how we do our business. Because we refer to it so much, we respectfully call it "The 45."

Because of the simplicity of the Napkin Presentations and the overall system, anyone can understand it and immediately put it into practice. It is because we used this concept of building an organization with depth that we have achieved such great success.

Many thanks to the Faillas for their expertise and knowledge that they've put into this book!

**– Willie and Dede Ashley**

I began a home-based business because of Don Failla's book. I have used this book as a tool for others I bring onto our team. I do not have to sit for hours explaining how to build a business or that network marketing is not a pyramid scheme. I simply give them the book. If they read it, I know they are interested. If they don't, I move on. And the audio version is a great tool. It's easy for me to listen to while I'm driving for business or with the kids—I use it to refresh my memory often!

*– Shannon Struik*

Don Failla's book, The 45 Second Presentation that Will Change Your Life, is an essential tool for any network marketing organization. This book has revolutionized the concept of network marketing for many, many in the industry. I had a negative image of network marketing prior to reading this book. However, after reading it, I was able to understand the concepts and patterns of thought which provided me with the tools to set up a successful system. Because of this book, I've been able to establish a system, execute my business effectively and ensure its longevity.

Teaching others the same system has launched my system forward. It makes the goal of building a network of people much more of a reality than I would have thought possible.

My business would not be what it is today without Mr. Failla's remarkable book. In fact, I would probably not have given network marketing a chance as a career. Of course, I have everyone that joins my network team read the book because I know it will give them the guidance the need to be successful. I can't think of a better gift!

*– Tiffany Obar*